TINA MODOTT

Mildred Constantine

A FRAGILE LIFE

CHRONICLE BOOKS

Library of Congress Cataloging-in-Publication Data
Constantine, Mildred.
    Tina Modotti: a fragile life / Mildred Constantine. -- New ed.
        p.   cm
    ISBN: 0-8118-0502-6 : $18.95
    1. Modotti, Tina, 1896-1942.   2. Photographers--Mexico--Biography.
I. Title.
TR140.M58C66   1993
770'.92--dc20
[B]   93-1154
                                                              CIP

Designed by Massimo Vignelli, New York
Typeset by Candice Odell, New York
Printed in Hong Kong.

Distributed in Canada
by Raincoast Books
112 East Third Avenue
Vancouver, B.C. V5T 1C8

10 9 8 7 6 5 4 3 2 1

Chronicle Books
275 Fifth Street
San Francisco, CA 94103

Cover: Tina, by Johan Hagemeyer, 1921 or 1922
Collection: The Bancroft Library, University
of California, Berkeley

Contents

Preface to New Edition   9

Acknowledgments   10

Introduction   11

: **1896/1923** Italy: Udine: USA: San Francisco, Los Angeles   19

: **1923/1926** Mexico: The Legend of Tina and Weston   61

: **1926/1930** Mexico: Commitment to Revolution; Expulsion   93

: **1930/1939** Germany, The Soviet Union, Spain   159

: **1939/1942** Refuge in Mexico   185

List of Illustrations   192

Bibliography   194

Footnotes   195

Index   196

For my daughters Judith and Vicki

We know the beginning of Tina Modotti's life in Italy; we know her sad end in Mexico. There is, however, no end to Modotti's story; it has been slowly unfolding.

I met Tina Modotti in Mexico in 1941. This book was a long time in the making. Over the years I was trying to sort and store information, to put together the strands of her history, and to forge an independent identity for her. The major research for the book began in the early 1970s when I found people more forthcoming. Up until that time Tina Modotti was famous for having been ignored, her work known to a small number of appreciative colleagues and historians, her story obscured by farcical errors and rumors where facts were missing.

It's almost twenty years since the first edition of *Tina Modotti: A Fragile Life* introduced the public to the work of this gifted artist and shed light on her courageous life—a life that had few tranquil times, that took her from Italy to the United States, to Mexico, the country that nurtured her art, to Holland, Germany, the former Soviet Union, Spain, and her return to Mexico.

The second edition of the book appeared in the USA in 1983. It provided more answers to questions and revealed a larger body of photographs. Translations of the book have also appeared in Spanish and in Japanese.

A critic writing in 1977 said, after seeing only forty photographs in a New York exhibition, "there is certainly enough there to ensure Modotti a permanent place in the annals of photography." There is certainly enough in her life to secure her a permanent place in the annals of the contemporary history of her time: the development of her art and the social and political context that helped shape her self-definition.

Since the mid-eighties, Tina Modotti has been given international recognition through exhibitions in England and Italy. Seminars have been held devoted to her life and work; documentaries have been made and shown throughout Europe. Archives of documents and photographs are in Berlin, Mexico, and at The Getty Center for The History of Art and Humanities in Santa Monica, California.

Still there are periods in her life in which there is no information at all and questions remain. Why did she return to Mexico rather than to Russia? Was it her intention to return to photography after the tumultuous years in Russia and Spain? Before she left for Spain, she had a new camera, a Leica, and had sold or exchanged her Graphlex. We know she didn't take the Leica to Spain, but rather left it with a young Italian friend in Moscow.

What are the overlooked spaces that Tina Modotti dwelled in of which we are still ignorant? The life of Tina Modotti discloses the flowering of the "firm and delicate being" whose memorable images illuminate the lives and cultures of the people in them as well as her own.

Mildred Constantine
1993

Acknowledgments

I wish to acknowledge with deep gratitude the knowledge, generosity, and encouragement, of the people who have helped to turn a legend into a portrait of a woman.

This book is based partly on interviews with people who knew Tina Modotti and whose memories served me well: Manuel Alvarez Bravo, Anita Brenner, Isabel Carbajal, Jean Charlot, Emily Edwards, Jay Leyda, Rosendo Gómez Lorenzo, Yolanda Magrini, Federico Marín, Pablo O'Higgins, Carlos Orozco Romero, María Marín de Orozco, Gustavo Ortiz Hernán, Victor Velarde and Vittorio Vidali. Vidali and Yolanda Magrini have also contributed documents, memorabilia, and photographs, the Weston archives, now in the Center for Creative Photography, Tucson, Arizona, holds the original letters from Tina to Edward Weston from which I have quoted; Cole and Neil Weston have been helpful and cooperative. Ben Maddow has been a profound inspiration in the writing of this work. Alastair Reid has written the beautiful translation of a section of Pablo Neruda's poem. Arthur A. Cohen and Eve Arnold have read the manuscript and provided more detached criticism than I could ever have made.

Ralph W. Bettelheim, my husband, whose spirit and wisdom accompanied me from the moment we both discovered the first firm thread of Tina's life, deserves most of my thanks for his patience and devotion to this work.

M. C.

...he was not a leader but she lived with direction and goal; she was not a woman who changed history but she always was at the center of a drama. She seems, whether in pleasure or in anguish, to have had a secret instinct for the limelight.

...there is a public image of Tina Modotti, it is based on gossipy notations of a few chroniclers offering mere notoriety. To certain brief acquaintances, Tina Modotti is known only as the apprentice, model and mistress of the great American photographer Edward Weston. A great and flamboyant beauty, a woman of many loves and numerous escapades, she was proclaimed a great mystery.

...met Tina Modotti for the first and only time in 1941. A close American friend, a Quaker living in Mexico, invited me to a meeting of the *Alianza Antifascista Giuseppe Garibaldi* and casually mentioned that we would have coffee with Tina Modotti after the meeting. I do not know what image of her I had conjured up in my own mind. When we shook hands and she welcomed me in English I was overwhelmed.

...had prepared myself for this meeting. I knew something of her story: that she had been expelled from Mexico; that she had lived in the Soviet Union; that she had been in Spain all during the Civil War; and that she had returned to Mexico with her companion Carlos Contreras, whom I had met on a separate occasion. She was a small, fragile, silent woman. I hardly dared to ask the many questions I had about her photography. I did not feel that her silence was born either of serenity or timidity, but that she seemed tragically tired. I could see the beauty I had been prepared for in spite of what seemed to be an anguished look in her eyes. The meeting did little more for me than to give Tina Modotti a face and compound the mystery of her.

...ot long after this meeting, my American friend wrote to tell me that Tina had died. She cautioned me not to believe rumors I might hear, and sent me a brochure printed in Mexico after Tina's death. This brochure yielded some facts hitherto unknown to me and enlarged on other information.

Tina was an Italian who had come to the United States in 1913.
Tina had been married to an American.
Tina had been an actress in Hollywood.
Tina had been Weston's apprentice, model and companion and they had lived in Mexico from 1923 to 1926.
Tina had been the companion of a Cuban, Julio Antonio Mella, who had been assassinated in Mexico.
Tina was expelled from Mexico in 1930.

Tina had been in the Soviet Union.
Tina had been in Spain — known as María — during the Spanish Civil War
from 1935 to 1939.
Tina had returned to Mexico in 1939 and died there in 1942.

Her name and some of her photographs had been known to me even before my
first visit to Mexico in 1936. The Mexican artists who were at work in
New York on the Federal Arts Project mural had told me of their program of
murals for public buildings which had begun in the early 1920's. Through
the magazine *Mexican Folkways*, I had seen photographs by Tina Modotti of
some of these painted walls. These compositions were impressive, as
were her photographs of Mexican children, colonial sculpture and folk art.

My primary reason for going to Mexico was the pursuit of my graduate studies
in Mexican colonial art. In retrospect I realize that this was also to be my first
adventure out of my own country and that I too was on a search. The modern
Mexico I encountered revealed a cultural and social current that astonished
me. I was little prepared for the unity of spirit I found there. It was inevitable
given the times and social conditions in the United States, that I should
respond to the aesthetic and political convictions expressed by the people I
encountered and by the modern Mexican art movement. With great alacrity
I abandoned the old and tried to absorb the new; it was not the colonial
past but the dramatic present that stirred my imagination and interest.

Arriving at the height of the second surge of mural art in Mexico, I eagerly
sought out the artists engaged in this work. David Alfaro Siqueiros was
in Spain — the Civil War had begun and he was among the first to volunteer.
Diego Rivera was too inaccessible to an art history student, in spite of the fac
that while on the staff of the College Art Association I had helped to organize
a defense of the Detroit murals. Not daring to use the camera myself, I tried t
find Tina Modotti or someone who knew her work. I made inquiries of friends:
Frances Toor, the editor of *Mexican Folkways*, Pablo O'Higgins and Leopoldo
Méndez, both artists who were engaged in the mural movement and also
working with the *Talleres de Gráfica Popular,* and Gustavo Ortíz Hernán, who
was then on the staff of the newspaper *El Universal.* All I could learn was that
Modotti was no longer in Mexico. There was mention of her being somewhere
in Europe. There were also stories of her having been a Hollywood actress wh
had lived in Mexico with Edward Weston (a name only vaguely known to
me at that time), and of her numerous lovers, although they were never named
Almost everyone mentioned her beauty, although no one seemed to have
a photograph of her. In the Rivera murals in Chapingo I could see the panels
"Virgin Soil" and "Life and Earth" for which she had been the model. The
stories were not like the tales of rumormongers, which always seem to be

plete with more information — fact or fiction. The legend of Tina Modotti
egan at that time.

s I pursued my research into Mexican art of the twenties I kept encountering
na's work — photographs in the book on Rivera's frescoes, Carleton Beals's
ticle in *Creative Arts*. I had no idea of her age, or of her nationality, or of her
ce. She had simply become part of the mythology of the modern Mexico
at I was trying to investigate.

ne years since my first visit had been filled with more work and travel
 Mexico, with participating in the excitement of the New Deal; my growing
olitical consciousness brought me to work for the Loyalists in the Spanish
vil War and other anti-Fascist causes. Then in 1946 the first major exhibition
 Edward Weston's photographs was held at the Museum of Modern Art in
ew York. Included were some splendid romantic photographs of Tina's hands
d her beautiful strong face. By 1949 I was at work at the Museum of
odern Art, and fortunate enough to be again under the guidance of René
Harnoncourt, then the Director. I had known him since the early thirties,
nen he brought a fine exhibition of Mexican art to the United States, and had
arned much from him about Mexican culture of the past as well as the
esent. He had lived and worked in Mexico during the exciting twenties, and
d met Weston and Modotti in 1925. He was convinced of the greatness
 Weston's work and of Tina's sure, growing talent. He too had heard of her
ath and of those vague rumors. The Museum had begun to acquire prints
 Weston's work, and in the late fifties several by Tina had come into the
llection. When the first volume of Weston's Daybooks was published in 1961,
avidly read his almost day-by-day account of those years in Mexico.
mehow the veil had been lifted only enough to make me more curious
out this woman. There was enough information about her to make
 know that there had been a major shift in values from those she had
nen she came to Mexico in 1923.

1971 I embarked on a search for Tina Modotti's photographs for a projected
hibition of her work at the Museum of Modern Art. This led me to
search for the story of her life. Not too surprisingly, Mexico in 1971 was far
fferent from the disputatious and divided Mexico of 1941. Thirty years
d softened attitudes, and people were more willing — even eager — to
minisce about the past. It is impossible to account for or to intuit
e whole of Tina's life. Yet I found, as I retraced my own past in the world
 Mexico's artists and intellectuals, that I could jog many memories
 that safely distant period.

y searches were based on a few questions: what are the facts, what are the mysteries in the life of Tina Modotti? How was she different from other women of her time? What control did she have over her own destiny and those close to her? What motivated the human and political feelings that find such rich expression in her work? And what about the multitudinous rumors about her death: that she had been killed in a car in Mexico; that she had been poisoned; that she had left the Soviet Union for Rumania and was murdered there; that she had been purged in Moscow in the thirties?

The world of art is indeed a very small one, and I found that my life since the early thirties had been touched by many of the same people who knew Tina Modotti.

Each person I interviewed led me to another. I dispatched a letter to Vittorio Vidali (whom I had known in Mexico as Carlos Contreras) in Trieste, where he has been living since the late forties. He generously gave me documents, newspaper clippings and photographs hitherto unknown to me. He also shared his knowledge and memories of his dead companion. He sent me on to Udine where Tina was born. There the *Circolo Culturale* had reprinted the brochure originally published in Mexico with additional photographs. I went back to the United States to meet Yolanda Magrini, Tina's youngest sister, who is living in California. Yolanda is the last of the Modotti family, and she gave me complete access to family photographs as well as her memories of her childhood.

Returning to Mexico, and now armed with more information, I again met with Manuel Alvarez Bravo, Anita Brenner, Federico Marín, María and Carlos Orozco Romero, Fernando Gamboa, Angélica Arenal de Siqueiros, Gustavo Ortíz Hernán, and Gómez Lorenzo.

The archives of the newspaper *Excelsior* were made available to me so that I could follow the day-by-day reporting on the assassination of Mella. Ben Maddow in Los Angeles was at work on his brilliant biography of Edward Weston. He not only helped to clarify salient points, but also made available to me copies of many letters Tina had written to Weston.

Each day brought a new clue; an unexpected chain of information grew. People seemed happy to know that Tina Modotti might be "resurrected" and recognized for herself and her work. In spite of the fact that many imponderables remained, I began to put the jigsaw of her life together.

Tina Modotti was a vital spirit in one of the most creative and evocative periods of the twentieth century. She was a woman created by many forces. She was a force in the life of a great photographer as well as a highly talented photographer in her own right. Yet her work is known and recognized by only

small number of appreciative colleagues and historians. Seen up to
now only through a shimmering veil, the woman Tina Modotti deserves to be
brought sharply into focus, to be revealed as the gifted artist and the
ardent revolutionary. I now feel that the veil has been lifted on that "fragile"
life of iron!

Mildred Constantine

1

1896/1923 Italy: Udine
USA: San Francisco, Los Angeles

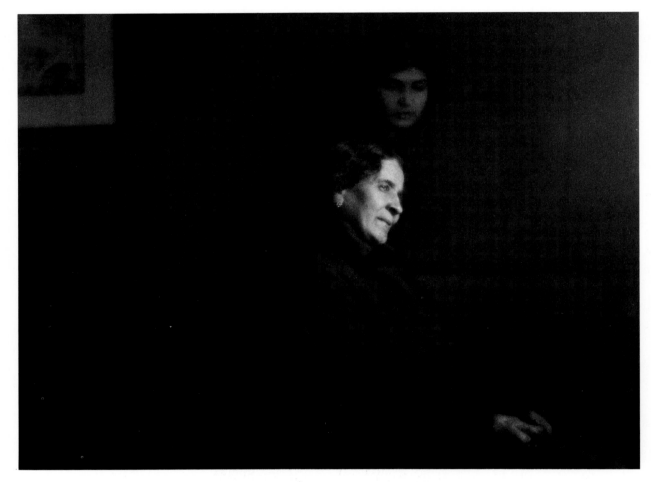

Tina and Mother, San Francisco, by Edward Weston, 1922
Collection: Mr. and Mrs. Ralph W. Bettelheim, New York

Passport No. 23.922 was issued in Barcelona, Spain, on December 21, 1937. It described the holder — Dra. Carmen Ruiz Sánchez — as a widow, professor by profession, with brown eyes, brown hair and oval face. This passport, valid for France, was renewed in Barcelona on January 21, 1939, marked for "*todo mundo*" except Germany, Italy, Portugal, Austria and Hungary. The woman was fleeing from Spain. She traveled from Figueras on February 3, 1939, France with a visa from the Agence Consular de France. There she received visa dated March 15, 1939, from the Mexican Legation in Paris. An American transit visa was given to her by the American consulate in Paris on March 27, allowing her to disembark on arrival in New York. Sailing from Cherbourg on the Queen Mary on April 1, she was denied permission, despite the transit visa, to disembark in New York. Finally, on April 19, 1939, she arrived at Vera Cruz, Mexico.

Tina Modotti was returning to Mexico with absolutely authentic false papers, a little less than ten years after being expelled. She was returning to the country that had been "home" for almost a decade of her brief, intense and creative life. This hegira from war-torn Spain to asylum in the revolutionary Mexico of President Lázaro Cárdenas was one of many she had been forced to make in her life. How many times in a lifetime can you begin to live?

Tina Modotti was many things: a gifted photographer, passionate companion of artists and revolutionaries, fighter for the cause of humanity, "María" who succored the children and wounded in Spain, the tempestuous beauty of unabashed sensuality. Who was she? Dead, she is a legend poeticized and victimized by conjecture, anecdotes and, where fact is lacking, imaginative embellishments.

It is difficult — almost impossible — to reconcile the woman Tina Modotti with the picture conjured up by those who knew her slightly, who freely gossiped and drew verbal pictures that are part of the literature and legends about her. That she was beautiful all agree.

Yet nothing so aggravated Tina as the references to her beauty. That she was aware of it one can be sure; it probably was her immediate passport into the Hollywood scene of 1920. On the other hand, she always had a sense of personal identity, and the Hollywood image of her as "femme fatale" suited neither her innate sense of dignity nor her earnest desire to be an actress. That she was able to arouse admiration, passion and desire in men is not surprising. That she was able to arouse admiration for her beauty in the women whom she met is both a tribute to her and to them. Apparently, it did not obscure their perception of her talent as an artist or her strength and honesty as a woman.

19

Tina, Udine, Age 4

As Tina's revolutionary awareness grew and she came increasingly to identify herself with political action, so, it seems, grew her resentment against those who spoke of her beauty. She was to state at the time of her deportation, "I could not possibly see what 'prettiness' had to do with the revolutionary movement. . . evidently women here [New Orleans] are measured by a motion picture star standard." Obviously her earlier Hollywood experience still rankled. In the many photographs Edward Weston made of Tina, the tempestuous beauty which Kenneth Rexroth claimed for her hardly appears. *There was a cafe where they all hung out with heavily armed politicians, bullfighters, criminals, prostitutes and burlesque girls. The most spectacular person of all was a photographer, artist's model, high class courtesan, and Mata Hari for the Comintern, Tina Modotti. She was the heroine of a lurid political assassination and was what I guess is called an international beauty. I had outgrown my fondness for the Kollantai type and she terrified me. She was exterminated in the Great Purge.*[1]

Aleksandra Mikhailovna Kollantai was a Russian revolutionist. She traveled internationally on propaganda missions which kept her away from her own country until the 1917 revolution, when she returned to assume a diplomatic post. She was a USSR minister to Mexico until 1928 (did she and Tina ever meet?). She was a proponent, in her novels and in her life, of a single standard of morality for men and women.

Rexroth was writing of a time in the late 1920's when he was in Mexico. In one paragraph he invented facts to suit his own fancy or need for fictionalizing events which happened long after his brief observations of this woman. Unhappily, later writers have often injudiciously quoted the Kollantai reference. And facts give the lie to his wishful inventions. Yet one person's malice often suffices to reinforce misconceptions and create a myth.

There is no fully detailed tapestry of the life of Tina Modotti. It cannot be unraveled, examined, evaluated. Facts, like bits of string, must first be entwined, and the lengths of twine must be overlapped and thickened to provide the rich warp and weft of her life. What are the implications of her strong yet vulnerable gaze, of her unrepressed sexuality, of the perseverance and fatalism which did not permit her to be reconciled to her own fate or to that of humanity?

She was a woman, she was an Italian. She did not set out to be a radical nonconformist. There was a personal, aesthetic and political order to the life of Tina Modotti. Each part had a specific shape. Each part was wedded to the other by her commitments. She chose to identify herself with the arts, with the poor and with the solidarity of the revolution. Instinct and upbringing, with rites and rituals, and the fact of her birthplace had prepared her for all that. ¬deniable intelligence and fortitude directed her ambitions and helped to ·eate the vital points of relationship between Tina and society.

ssunta Adelaide Luigia Modotti — always called Tina — was born in Udine, ¬ly, on August 16, 1896. Udine, the capital of the province of Friuli, is ∣tuated at the foot of the Alps. Its location northeast of Venice makes it a ∣rategic point between the approach to the Adriatic on the south and to ∣ustria on the north. It has a profoundly Latin population and at the time of ¬na's birth had a predominantly feudal society with a long history of ·cial unrest. It is a medieval city of classical palaces, piazzas, fountains, ¬cient markers with roads and streets that run up to the hills. Udine's ∣imate and the vegetation in the mountains and hills encourage extensive ¬d cultivation. The Friuliani are hard-working, hard-playing people. ¬ey are passionate, yet not as garrulous as most other Italians. One feels they ·e a people of an ancient and civilized heritage.

this small, peaceful town, the people knew intimately the section in which ·ey lived. Democracy was at work in the schools, at play in the streets and the taverns. The houses, mainly sixteenth- and seventeenth-century buildings, ·re lived in by a cross-section of the population. Those of wealth and social ¬nding lived in the *piano nobile* (palatial floor) of these old houses, while ·e tradesmen and artisans lived, together with their families, in their shops on ·e ground level. One was always aware of the countryside. Vegetable and ∣wer gardens flourished; roads led gently toward the hills or to the center of ∣wn. There was communion in the streets: the children of all families ·tended the same schools (if indeed they went to school) and played together the streets. On Sundays the workers' families and children were all ·essed in their finery and indistinguishable from the more bourgeois ∣wnsfolk. The women met to do their laundry in the public canals, ¬d the men gathered in the taverns.

∣e ordinary working man searched his way through many paths, eagerly ¬bracing the essential contradictions in his life. He was generally poor but ∣ogressive, and maintained an inner dignity. Those who did not till the soil ∣rked as carpenters, blacksmiths and bricklayers. When such work was ∣arce, they would go out for seasonal work. They went out because of need, ·cause of tradition, but they also went with pride and with hope for ·eir future.

∣ instinct of class, a Friuliano was a socially conscious being — a ∣volutionary through the Socialist party. He would have had contact with labor ∣ruggles through his proximity to Austria and to the industrialization going

Benvenuto Modotti, Tina's brother, Udine, by P. Modotti, c. 1915. Perhaps a relative who interested Tina in the camera.

21

Tina, San Francisco, c. 1918–20

on in the province of Lombardy. Tina's youngest sister, Yolanda, relates Tina's nostalgic memories of her childhood, when her father carried her on his shoulders as he participated in the noisy May Day demonstrations.

Giuseppe Modotti and his wife Assunta lived with their six children: the girls, Mercedes, Tina, Yolanda, Giaconda; the boys, Benvenuto and Giuseppe. Of this family only Yolanda Magrini remains. Yolanda is a tiny, spirited, beautiful seventy-two-year-old woman who lives in a plant- and flower-filled home in southern California. She is still the politically aware and active representative of her family tradition.

Seeking work in Austria, Giuseppe moved his family there for several years. They remained there until Tina was nine years old. Returning to Udine, Tina's father continued to work as a mason. When he had saved enough money he left his family behind and emigrated to the United States, settling in San Francisco. Tina, the second eldest child, worked in a textile factory to help support her mother and the younger children.

According to Paul Radin, writing in 1935, the Italian coming to California experienced less discrimination in the nineteenth century than other minority groups which had arrived during the mining days. Andrew Rollo, writing in 1968, also described life for the Italians who went West as neither disappointing nor miserable. "In general, there were no slums, crowding and little prejudice." According to Rollo, the Italian colony was self-sufficient to a large degree "partly because it wanted to be and partly because it was constrained to be."

Rollo says that Italian immigrants maintained strong family ties and habitually married within their own groups. There was little change of occupation or uprooting of the values inculcated in Italy. Bakeries, groceries, banks, cafes, restaurants, lawyers, were all in the self-contained world of little Italy. Of the almost 17,000 Italians in San Francisco, over half were northern Italians. They had their own newspapers and, by the 1900's, their own theatrical groups, opera companies. While they were considered active participants in the life of the city, they constituted a world unto themselves.

On the other hand, it is acknowledged that well before the United States entered World War I, workers' conditions in California were extremely bad. Over-long working hours and bad housing facilities created strikes which brought violence from both sides.

Giuseppe Modotti, having had contact with the labor struggles in Italy, was certainly responsive to the conditions of workers who, like himself, had been

eglected by the craft unions and were laboring under unfair conditions. The
alians in California found that almost everything grown in the old country
uld be grown in San Francisco, and the importance of San Francisco as a
cific port was greatly increased by the Spanish-American War. Still, artisans
ch as carpenters and masons were no more secure as wage-earners than
ey had been in Italy.

evertheless, the eldest daughter was able to join her father, and by 1913
iuseppe Modotti had earned enough money to send for Tina, who left
California in a third-class boat full of Italian immigrants. She was just
venteen years old. Removal to a new world did not alter the need to
ork — or her will to do so. About a week after arrival in San Francisco, she
gan to work in a textile factory. What life was like after the entire family
d finally emigrated to San Francisco several years later is best described by
r youngest sister, Yolanda. She recalls, in speaking of Tina:

*hen she was only a young girl, she looked to me, younger as I was, like a
tle lady, with those big, sad eyes in a hunger-stricken face. She was the only
e among the six of us who worked and made a few pennies a day. She
ed to work twelve hours a day in a silk factory, and whatever her duties were,
r fingers were always swollen and sore. One night, in early winter, our
e and candles had gone out, as it would often happen. My mother and I
re waiting for Tina, clinging to each other in order to keep warm. We
re sad and dejected because there was nothing to eat. When we would have
od, I would run to meet Tina, anxious to tell her the good news.
ur main concern throughout our childhood was to have something to eat,
we did not have any toys and we could never find the time to enjoy ourselves.
ur youngest brother would often cry when, back from school, he would realize
it there was nothing to eat; but Tina never said anything, quietly going to bed
ht after coming home from work...*

Tina and Robo with his family, Los Angeles, 1921

en as a young child in Italy, and later in the United States, Tina was
dowed with a deep sense of responsibility toward her family. Leaving the
tory to seek more remunerative work, she turned to dressmaking and
de deliveries for additional income.

spite of the poverty, long hours of work, the insufficiency of food, this
riod of life in the United States opened many new directions for Tina. The
man's suffrage movement from 1910 onward gave women new freedom
function outside the household. This new atmosphere obviously encouraged
na's independence, and she began to take part in amateur theatrical
tivity in the Italian quarter. Her father was an amateur musician and he
o participated in the theater and street fiestas. René Dubos has
itten that San Francisco

...developed without Puritan influence. However, it was soon given a special character by the large number of immigrants who came to it from northern Ital *Unlike poor Sicilians and Neapolitans, these north Italians had a great awareness of European culture and created an atmosphere similar to that of cosmopolitan Mediterranean harbors but without the Mediterranean poverty... Not having arisen as a WASP settlement, San Francisco acquired from the beginning the mood of a large European continental city, with sections where anybody could engage in behavior of his own choice, no matter how far out. Indifference toward conventional mores and openness to cultural innovatio* *made it a mecca for persons in search of new life styles...*[2]

Perhaps it was the general as well as a personal search for a new direction in her life that prompted Tina to fall in love with an American poet and painter French Canadian background. Roubaix de L'Abrie Richéy was tall, slender, with a dark moustache and large eyes. We know little about him except that h came from a large family which had been in America for over a generation and had resided first in New Orleans, and then in Los Angeles. They met, Yolanda recalls, at a function at the Pan Pacific International Exposition in San Francisco in 1915.

Approximately two years later they were married and moved to Los Angeles, setting up their home in Richéy's studio. Tina ever the conscientious wage-earner, continued her dressmaking. Richéy pursued his painting and hi poetry, but with an uncertainty about both activities. Was this marriage a way out of Tina's particular ghetto, and did she hope through it to assimilate herse into American life? What insight we have into Richéy is gained from the love photograph which Weston made. This picture captures perfectly the romantic aura which surrounded him. The flowing tie, the shy, downward, indirect gaze the hands and only part of the face illuminated, confirm Tina's own descriptio of him:

Roubaix de L'Abrie Richéy (Robo)

...a young boy with eyes dimmed by dreams...overwhelmed by that vague "something" which is present at all times for the soul sensitive enough to percei it. And it was no doubt the overpowering force of his sensitive emotions and sensibilities that made him turn to art and pursue it as an outlet and a means expression. As he grew up, all his artistic fervor pervaded his whole being and personality. All of himself was his personality...he always attracted attention for his simple charm and gentle manners. Never part of a crowd nor happy amid one, he was at his best in the company of a few intimate and sympathetic friends.[3]

Tina herself was not content to remain a dressmaker. Whether it was through her earlier experience as an amateur actress that she was "discovered" by the Hollywood film world is not entirely certain. We know that she was ambitious

Tina and Robo at home, Los Angeles, 1921

and interested in dramatics, and it must have been logical, given her beauty, to seek a future in Hollywood. Certainly her search for self-expression might have found an outlet in acting, and it was a profession more lucrative than dressmaking. Her beauty, acknowledged by all who knew her, must have given her access to Hollywood. In later years, as she became Weston's model, she must have been aware of the electrifying effect her beauty had on those around her. Did she consciously make use of this power? We have already seen how even women commented on and enjoyed her beauty and how, as her political awareness grew, her abhorrence of references to her beauty was readily expressed.

However Tina entered the world of Hollywood, in 1920 she was featured in several films. She was always costumed as a gypsy or harem girl, in the typical Hollywood version of the female "heavy" of the era. But this typecasting did not appeal to Tina. "The exotic allure of Tina Modotti," proclaimed in a poster for *The Tiger's Eye* (1920), exploited nothing more than her physical attributes. This crude exploitation was limiting and offensive to both her dignity and her aspirations. As Weston put it when they happened upon one of her films in Mexico, "We had a good laugh over the villainous character she portrayed. The brains and imaginations of our movie directors cannot picture an Italian girl except with a knife in her teeth and blood in her eye."[4]

The post-war period in Los Angeles saw a clash between the smugness of the people who carried on the old traditions those who sought the new. The different strata of people ranged from those who had carried their midwestern habits with them, to the new immigrants, to those who were pioneering and hoped to find fertile ground for their ideas.

This photograph and the nine that follow are of Tina in Hollywood, 1920–21

Robo's studio (her husband was called Robo by all who knew him) was something of a gathering place for bohemian writers and artists with radical points of view. All had in common the need to attack the status quo of the time. They sought personal and sexual independence as a requisite to artistic expression, and carried on endless discussions about contemporary music, dance, literature and art. Together they explored psychoanalysis, socialism, and the religious movements — from Hinduism to Christian Science — which had begun to take root in Los Angeles. They banded together to make each feel that he was not alone and not simply floating through life. They cooly indulged in appraising each other, in self-expression and drinking in the complexities of the times — of Joyce, Pound, Freud — with a restless vitality.

Among those who met in the Richéys' studio in 1921 were Ramiel McGehee, a writer; Sadakichi Hartmann (Sidney Allen), a film and photography critic; Edward Weston, photographer; Margrethe Mather, photographer; and the

Mexican archaeologist Ricardo Gómez Robelo, who was at that time head of the Fine Arts Department of Mexico. Other Mexican artists and intellectuals were frequent guests as well, and they brought stimulating reports of the reemergence of the Mexican Indian past and the exciting possibilities offered by the revolution of their day — a revolution expressed in cultural as well as social terms. In response to an invitation from Gómez Robelo, Robo left in December 1921 for Mexico, where he hoped to find an environment better suited to his temperament. As Tina was to write so movingly after Robo's death: "With an intentional disregard for the modern spirit of this age and of this country in particular (the United States), attracted by the beauty and the charm of the past still lingering there...he found sympathy and romance...but only for a little while."[5]

Whether it was through McGehee's contacts with the movie colony, as suggested by Ben Maddow, that Weston first met Tina, a "truly extraordinary woman who was to shatter and then reconstruct his life" (Introduction, Daybook No. 1), or whether their first meeting took place in Robo's studio is not certain.

We do know from a letter which Tina wrote to Weston on April 25 of that same year that their affair had begun before Robo had left for Mexico. In the letter Tina had written, "One night after — all day I have been intoxicated with the memory of last night and overwhelmed with the beauty and madness of it...How can I wait until we meet again!" That this affair was adulterous for both Tina and Weston did not lessen the beauty; indeed it contributed to the madness. In a response to one of Weston's letters, Tina said:
Once more I have been reading your letter and as at every other time my eyes are full of tears — I never realized before that a letter — a mere sheet of paper — could be such a spiritual thing — could emanate so much feeling — you gave a soul to it! Oh! If I could be with you now at this hour I love so much, I would try to tell you how much beauty has been added to my life lately! When may I come over? I am waiting for your call.

This is undoubtedly the first in the long series of letters which Tina and Weston exchanged. This communication is remarkable both for the unselfconscious passion, the exultant tasting of sensual experience, and the need she expressed.

In the photographs Weston made of Tina during this year one can see why. "Tina hit Edward like a tempest; she had about her a magnificence and a nobility no one who knew her could ever afterward forget."[6] But in that early time of their relationship Weston has also caught her rapt gaze and youthful passion. When Tina talks about "the beauty which has been added to my life,"

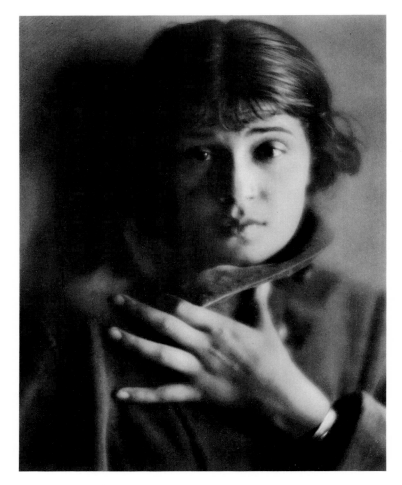

Tina, Los Angeles, by Edward Weston, 1921
Collection: Center for Creative Photography, Tucson, Arizona

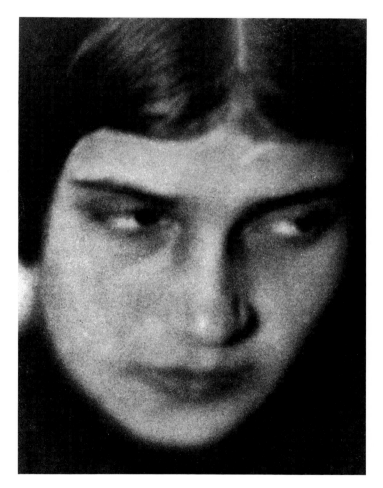

Tina, Los Angeles, by Edward Weston, 1921
Collection: Center for Creative Photography, Tucson, Arizona

Tina, Los Angeles, by Edward Weston, 1921
Collection: Center for Creative Photography, Tucson, Arizona

Next page:
Tina, Los Angeles, by Edward Weston, 1921
Collection: Center for Creative Photography, Tucson, Arizona

41

Assunta Modotti, Tina's mother, by Edward Weston, 1922

Tina, Glendale, by Edward Weston, 1922
Collection: Center for Creative Photography, Tucson, Arizona

it suggests that her love for Robo might have been unsatisfactory in some way, perhaps physically, and that their relationship, though not strained, was not as fulfilling as Tina had hoped. It also suggests an awareness of a change in her nature.

One might ask why it was Weston to whom Tina responded in so clear a way that the clandestine meetings were eagerly sought out by her, without any false modesty or reticence. Edward Weston, today regarded as one of America's greatest photographers, in 1921 was thirty-five years old, married, and the father of four boys. He had been in California since 1906 and was living in Glendale, a suburb of Los Angeles. He had been both a commercial and professional photographer, but even his commercial portraits bore evidence of a greatness to come. He had already been awarded prizes in exhibitions, and his work had been acclaimed by critics and by other photographers. Imogen Cunningham, herself a marvelous photographer, had written words of high praise for his work in 1920.

Weston is described by a friend as "not an imposing man; he was small but powerfully built, nor was he, in fact, particularly handsome." Soft-voiced and gentle, he was nonetheless an extrovert. He had had very little formal education; "his remarkable and acute intelligence was simply directed another way."

Growing up in the Midwest, Weston had been raised by a sister and an aunt, his mother having died when he was only five years old. His addiction to photography started in 1902, when his father, a doctor, gave him a Bulls-Eye camera for his sixteenth birthday. Although he later worked for Marshall Field & Company in Chicago, with surveyors on railroads in Los Angeles and Nevada, as a house-to-house professional portrait photographer, he knew from the start the profound meaning that the art of photography held for him.

His marriage to Flora May Chandler, a close friend of his sister, was in many ways a throwback to his proper Midwest upbringing, and they had four sons. By 1921, when he met Tina, he had abandoned his commercial success and begun experimenting in photography. He had become increasingly discontent with the strictures of family life; his relationship with his wife had deteriorated over the years, and he had had numerous affairs. On the other hand, his relationship with his sons was constant and profound, a responsibility he eagerly accepted.

Weston's was a constant battle against poverty. He had to support himself, to support his belief in his art, and to contribute to the support of his family. His wife, a teacher, was the financial mainstay of the household. But Weston

o pursued a separate existence, spending much of his time with his
oup — McGehee, Mather, and Johan Hagemeyer, another photographer —
rty-going, attending concerts, drinking wine and enjoying endless discussions.

fe in the Weston household in Glendale must have been madly inhibiting,
d the atmosphere of Robo's studio provided a haven for him and his group.
e wonder whether Robo's family had helped to contribute toward the security
d comfort of Robo and Tina, since the meetings of friends there might have
ovided comradeship as well as a sense of well-being.

hy did Tina fall in love with Weston at this time of her life? She was
enty-five years old and involved in a conscious search for direction in her
e. Hollywood provided no answer — it demeaned her intentions. She was
schooled but immensely curious about the intellectual world. Here was an
der, more sophisticated man who had temperament and background so
like her own — and probably unlike that of Robo (Weston often proclaimed
mself to be 100 per cent American). He was a man who used sexuality as a
eans of self-expression and liberation, a man with a single-minded devotion
his art. He would allow neither himself nor his art to be betrayed by
nvention. His virility and physicality, which are generally acknowledged,
ust have electrified Tina. Although we have no evidence, we might assume
na's sexual inexperience up to this time.

obo's uncertainty and timidness about himself and about his work; Tina's
sappointment with Hollywood and its disregard of her desire to act; probably
r own searching and seeking a useful and creative life — all these factors
ust have contributed to her enchantment with Weston and his group. She
anted to share in their excursions, explorations, discussions. Her involvement
th these people may have provided a kind of education pointing a way to the
ture. It is perhaps for this reason that she also sought the friendship of Johan
agemeyer, one of Weston's closest friends. Hagemeyer had known Weston
nce 1917 and had shared his devotion to photography and music. On August
, 1921, while visiting her family in San Francisco, Tina wrote to Hagemeyer:
*fore everything else, please excuse if I have misspelled your name as I fear I
ve. Mr. Weston gave me your address before leaving (or rather I asked him for
as I was looking forward to see you. He also told me of the good books and
usic you have (therefore my impertinence). I am only going to be here one week
ore, so any time it is convenient for you, please call me on the phone and I will
me over. My number is Franklin 9566 — about 9 o'clock in the morning is the
st time. Tina de Richéy.*

n September 16, Weston wrote to Hagemeyer from Los Angeles: "Tina goes to
exico very shortly — she wrote me and said 'I realized then how deep the

*By Giovanni Batista Pergolesi, 18th century composer.

friendship between J. H. and you must be — for in him there was so much that made me think of you — and again you remind me much of him. Thanking him for the precious afternoon is not enough — I must also tell you how much appreciated his cordial kindness and sympathetic company.'" Tina had obviously planned to go to Mexico to join Robo. There appears to have been rupture in their marriage, the affair with Weston being sporadic and perhaps at that time more a manifestation of their restlessness, a purely physical experience rather than a commitment. Tina cherished the exposure to books and music which Hagemeyer provided and perhaps also unconsciously sought a physical and intellectual closeness to him as a surrogate for Weston. She wrote again to Hagemeyer on September 17, from Los Angeles:

I have written you about a dozen letters in my mind but never have I been able put them into written form. Not for lack of thoughts — instead — the impressions left to me of the afternoon spent with you were so many and so deep they overwhelmed my mind. But here I am making a brave effort to express all I feel full well knowing it is futile — for not even to myself can I clearly answer why I suppressed the great desire I had to call on you once more. Was it power of will or was it cowardice? Maybe the same spirit moved me then, what moved Oscar Wilde to write this paradox. "There are only two tragedies in this world; one consists in not obtaining that which you desire; the other consists in obtaining it." The last one is the worst — the last is a real tragedy. And so I left without satisfying my desire of listening once more to Pergolesi's "Nina"* in your company. Since then I have played it twice — only twice — for I fear to play it oftener — and besides I must be alone when I listen to it — all alone — in order to give myself the illusion that I am not alone, nor here, but in 2616 Webster Street [Hagemeyer's old address]. Whether I will ever see you again or not, the brief b rich hours spent with you are the most precious to me and I will live them over with the same beauty and sadness of that day. Thanking you for the joy your books and music together with your sympathetic company have procured me. I have not seen your friend Edward since I returned, but he asked me to pose once more for him before leaving for Mexico. That made me very happy and filled me with pride. Oh! I hope he does something very great again! For his sake — as for me I cannot desire anything greater than what he has already done of me. Tina.

Several things, which we know only from Tina's writing, become evident in th correspondence. It is August 1921. The affair with Weston, having begun just four months ago, might appear to have been just an affair. Robo is still very much in the picture; he is not to leave until December of that year, and Tina has indicated that she plans to join him. This is not a spontaneous decision, but has been planned by both. Weston had made his first photographs of Tina and was eager to continue. Tina was fascinated by Weston and revered his work. It is even possible that Weston had already started aching Tina to use the camera. Maddow states that "she soon became his pupil, his model, his admirer, and his mistress: all three more or less at the same time."[7] For her their affair seems to have begun something that was more than a sexual adventure: Tina became aware of her own sexuality, and the possibilities of an independent future.

As we look at Weston's photographs of this period we see an extraordinarily beautiful woman, whose intense sexuality is perhaps heightened by her vulnerability. The photographs definitely belong to Weston's romantic period — the soft lens focusing on Tina's timid and youthful gaze, her face filled with the breath of love; they are more revealing of the sitter than were Weston's previous portraits. In her face is a subtlety and a hint of the dignity to come. The photograph on page 41 is one that is unknown to Weston's family and the historians of his art, but it must have had special meaning for Tina since it was in her possession up until her death and was used on her bier.

While there must also have been feelings of guilt on Weston's part because of his relationship with Tina, he and Robo remained friends. Two weeks after Robo arrived in Mexico, he wrote to Weston in glowing terms of this "land of extremes." He called it the artist's paradise, and said:

Here is little that is devoid of beauty. There is for me more poetry in one lone shrouded figure leaning in the door of the pulque shop at twilight or a bronzen daughter of the Aztecs nursing her child in a church than could be found in Los Angeles in the next ten years...Can you imagine an art school where everything is free to everyone — Mexicans and foreigners alike — tuition, board, room, paint, canvas, models, all free — no entrance examination — if one will study, that is the only requirement. After ten years of war and unrest it is wonderful to see what is being done here.

Robo described the landscape, the ancient cities and monuments, volcanoes, and the many friends he had gained. He tried hard to persuade Weston to join him, and closed his letter, "Believe me to be as ever your friend, 'Robo.'" Robo became suddenly ill with smallpox, and after a brief but violent few days he died on February 9, 1922.

In a newspaper interview after his death and on the occasion of a posthumous exhibition of his paintings and batiks, some of which had been designed for her to wear in the movies, Tina stated: "We didn't even know it until toward the end. I was on a train going to him when I was handed a telegram — he was dead. I am thinking of him — dying alone, with no member of his family near him. It was terrible." He was thirty-one. In Tina's tribute to her husband she wrote, "Death came, swift and inexorable, and he vanished... from a world which he did not belong."

Self-portrait, by Johan Hagemeyer, 1921 (?)
Collection: The Bancroft Library, University of
California, Berkeley

Next page:
Tina, San Francisco, by Johan Hagemeyer, 1921 or 1922
Collection: The Bancroft Library, University of
California, Berkeley

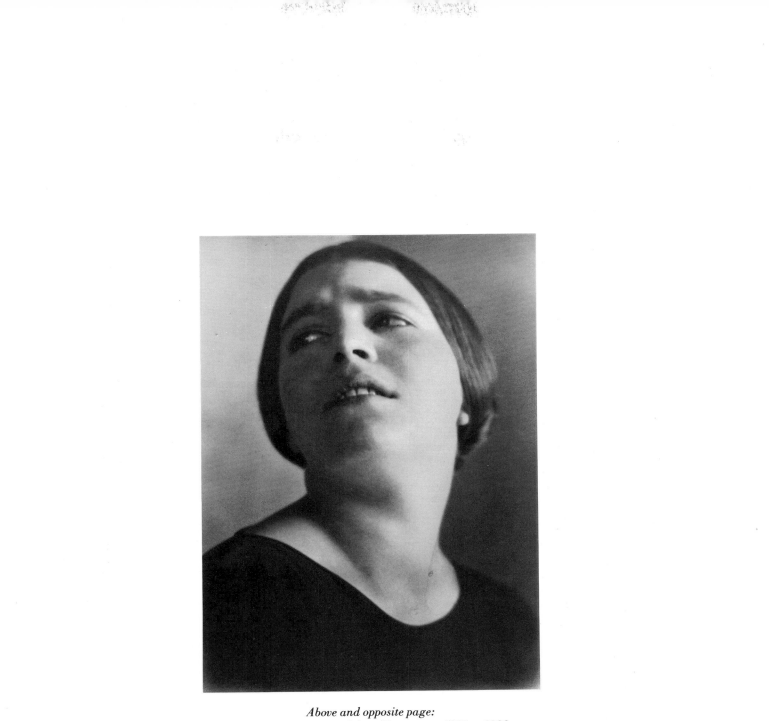

Above and opposite page:
Tina, San Francisco, Johan Hagemeyer, 1921 or 1922
Collection: The Bancroft Library, University of
California, Berkeley

Among the prose she selected for publication, Tina included Robo's "Words," in which he describes the personal significance which certain words have for him. To him "Robo is a rolling motion, as the waves in the ocean or the curved back of a brush"; "Tina is wine red and something very precious that one puts gently down to become more precious as they carefully put it down."

These words may indicate Robo's awareness that Tina was growing away from him toward Weston. He may reluctantly have acknowledged that he was destined to lose Tina. Did his knowledge of the affair hasten his decision to accept the invitation to go to Mexico and look for a "sympathy and romance that he could no longer find in Los Angeles? We know from Tina's family that there was no estrangement between them, and that she had planned to join him. But, unfortunately, we have no record of letters that they may have exchanged during that period.

Tina herself must have felt some guilt, not only because of the affair with Weston but probably because of the emotions and passions that it had awakened in her. While there had been no explicit bourgeois rules of behavior in her upbringing, it is probable that up to the time of Weston Tina had observed the moral code of marriage. For his part, Weston had had other loves and other sexual adventures before Tina.

A sense of family was always very strong in Tina, and this had evidently extended to Robo's family as well, particularly in her relationship with Robo's mother. Emily Edwards, a writer, remarks in a letter: "Once I met the delicately beautiful woman who had been Tina's mother-in-law... his [Robo's] mother and Tina seemed to be tenderly fond of one another. They are so very different. The slim conventional older woman seemed the younger of the two — an ageless maturity was Tina's." Tina and Robo's mother went together to Mexico after Robo's death, and it was in Mexico that Tina sensed the challenging possibilities for the expansion of her own self.

She stayed for several weeks, discovering the stirring times, the glowing landscape, renewing her friendship with Robelo and meeting the many friends Robo had made. She had also brought several of Weston's photographs and found a warm response from Mexican artists and intellectuals when she arranged for a showing in the *Academia de Bellas Artes*. His work was a revelation for the Mexican artists, who had previously given photography little attention as an art form.

Tina went to Mexico in 1922, a year which saw a great resurgence of national pride: "Mexico for the Mexicans." Anita Brenner describes this period:
There was a lift, a stirring feeling in Mexico in the early twenties when the last

ief had made his arrangements with Obregón, and each agrarian cradled
is gun in some safe place, like the roofhatch. It was new, it was a spring world
here fear was skewered...there was a sense of strength released: much work
do, everything at the beginning...Artists returned from guerrilla trooping
nd from war-exhausted Europe; poets wrote lyrics, peasants humanized
actors with flowers and Indian nicknames for steam shovels.[8]

y 1921, President Obregón had reestablished a Ministry of Education
ith José Vasconcelos, who had returned from a five-year exile, as Minister.
asconcelos was highly enthusiastic about the cultural aspects of the
evolution, which would involve the contemporary artist in the life of the
ountry. He held to the thesis that the Indian should be "redeemed"
nd the masses educated. He had been a friend of Zapata and one-time
oldier with Pancho Villa. By providing them with commissions,
asconcelos enabled the artists to serve to their fullest abilities and without
deological censorship.

was this Mexico which Robo had glimpsed and which Tina now discovered
r herself. Painters in overalls were putting the meaning of the revolution
n public walls; they communicated with feeling and force what they had to
y. Critics from all over the world felt that this was the first great modern
rt to have been created in America.

*Robo's mother at his grave, Pantheon de Dolores,
Mexico, 1922*

he birth of a Mexican school of painters whose inspiration came from the
Iexican scene did not, however, occur overnight. Nor were the implications of
is phenomenon confined to the sphere of artistic activity. "The stirrings
f artistic revolt in Mexico preceded the political upheaval. In 1909 Dr. Atl, a
ioneer figure in the history of Mexican art, had begun to preach nationalism.
he following year, the students at the *Academia de Bellas Artes* (including the
oung David Alfaro Siqueiros) struck against the obsolete methods practiced
ere and walked out, never to return."[9]

rancisco Goitía and José Clemente Orozco were already independently
ointing the way to social paintings. They were joined later by a large group of
rt students in a revolt against the Huerta dictatorship. By 1919 a congress of
oldier-artists convened to plan new directions for art and for culture generally.
avid Alfaro Siqueiros and Carlos Orozco Romero were sent off to Europe
study; there, Siqueiros was to meet Diego Rivera. Their relationship was to
ave important repercussions for the developing arts in Mexico and for their
wn artistic development.

iego Rivera was in Paris during the important years of the Cubist period and
as associated with Braque, Klee and Picasso. In Italy he was much impressed

with the great frescoes, the Byzantine mural mosaics and the Etruscan relics that recalled the plastic strength of ancient Mexican art. He returned to Mexico in July 1921 to paint his first mural. David Alfaro Siqueiros had joined Carranza's revolutionary army in 1913, and was an active soldier until he left Mexico. While traveling in Europe, 1919 to 1922, he began to formulate his views on the artistic revolution, and he published a manifesto in Barcelona in May, 1921, stating for the first time his conception of monumental mural painting. Rivera and Siqueiros were to lead the Mexican artistic revolution and both were to figure largely in the life of Tina Modotti.

Together they organized the Revolutionary Syndicate of Technical Workers, Painters and Sculptors *(Sindicato de Técnicos, Pintores y Escultores)*. Their publication, *El Machete,* became the medium for proclaiming their aims. Speaking to the Mexican people, they declared solidarity in the effort to overthrow the old, inhuman system and to recognize the spiritual vitality of the race. They sought to restore the peculiar ability of the Mexican to create beauty through indigenous Mexican art. "It is great because it surges from the people; it is collective, and our own aesthetic aim is to socialize artistic expression, to destroy bourgeois individualism...We hail the monumental expression of art because such art is public property." Such was the manifesto issued by the *Sindicato* in 1922 (the year of Tina's first visit to Mexico), the time of Obregón presidency and the beginning of a tremendous program in the arts. Cultural activity was encouraged through a broad program of popular education, renewed interest in the popular arts, open-air schools, (about which Robo had reported glowingly in his letter to Weston).

The nationalistic movement in painting was leaving its mark on market places, government offices, churches and other public buildings. Mexican folk tunes and regional music and instruments came into fashion. Moreover, the renaissance was not limited to artistic activity. Women assumed a significant new place in society. They gained the right to vote and to participate in government and business. New educational opportunities, as well as coeducation, became available to them.

Mexico was indeed for the Mexicans, but they also gave asylum to political exiles from Central and South American countries and offered them jobs with the encouragement that their lives might take root in Mexico. Tina did not find this Mexico alien to her. She was moved by all she saw and by the promise of a future, and was determined to find a place for herself in the new Mexico - the Mexico of the revolution. Upon her return to San Francisco after the death of her father, in March of 1922, she again sought to renew the friendship with Johan Hagemeyer. Tina had already begun, as Weston's pupil, to use the camera. And the fact that Hagemeyer was a photographer, an intellectual

d an anarchist born in Europe must certainly have provided another bond in
eir friendship. She wrote to him shortly after her return, on April 7, 1922:
*hesitated long whether to get in touch with you or not for I had made it my
ogramme before coming here not to see anyone outside of my family. But the
her day — finding myself alone — an uncontrollable desire came upon me
hear "Nina" again. And so I did — and as I listened to it the agitated life of
ese past few months became dimmer and dimmer while the memory of a
rtain afternoon came back to me with all the illusion of reality — a certain
ternoon when for the first time that soul-torturing music took hold of me and
ft me a little sadder perhaps but with a richer soul. And because of all this I
el the desire to spend another afternoon with you — can the first ever be
uplicated? I fear not — but "Nina" at least will be the same. Can you drop me
card and let me know when I can call? I will remain here until Easter — fond
I am of this place — yet I am anxious to leave it — it holds too many memories
r me — here I live constantly in the past, and "Life," said George Moore,
s beautiful at the moment, but sad when we look back." For me life is always
d — for even in the present moment I feel the past. Mine must be a spirit of
cadence, and by living here I only give vent to it — but yet — I feel that only by
ing in the past can we revenge ourselves on nature — I wonder how you feel
out all this — perhaps we can talk it over. Cordially, Tina Modotti de Richéy.*

he loss of husband and father within a two-month period must have been
 attering to Tina. She often came to San Francisco to see her family; she even
ought about opening a photographic studio there. Hagemeyer might have
ovided a comforting friendship without the stress accompanying emotional
d physical involvement.

he affair with Weston was continuing, although it was not without its trials
d digressions. In early letters to Weston, Tina sounds as though she amazed
erself with the deepness of her love and felt elated to give unstintingly, ready
ot only for the elemental sexuality of their relationship, but also for the
eauty which it added to her life. She wrote to him in October 1922, when their
lationship seemed to be floundering, "Good-bye — good-bye Edward, may
ou attain all you deserve — but is that possible — you give so much — how can
ife' ever pay you back? I can only send a few rose petals and a kiss." (It
as to be several months before Weston and Tina left for Mexico, where they
arted their lives together.) It sounds as though Tina felt that their affair
as over, and in a letter to Hagemeyer in October she asked if he had heard
om Weston since his arrival in Ohio on a visit to his sister. Yet when
eston went to New York in November of that year, they obviously remained
touch. Weston noted in his Daybook (p. 10) that "Tina sent two 'specials,'
ach with $20 enclosed, knowing that I would need money; that I
ust see Balieff's 'Chauve Souris.'"

*The cover photograph and those on page 49, 50
and 51 were made by Johan Hagemeyer
undoubtedly on the occasion of one of Tina's
visits. These quiet and poignant images reflect a
remarkable insight and communication between
sitter and photographer.*

The photo on page 18 is the unpublished photograph of Tina and her mother by Weston. We can assume that it was done sometime in 1922. It establishes Weston's romantic response to the closeness of Tina and her mother. The asymmetrical composition, the background darkness, one figure almost lost in shadow but leaning over and touching the other; the illumination of the face and hands of the mother; all project a reverence for the harmony between daughter and mother.

Weston's involvement with Tina had by this time extended to her family as well, and he was warmly welcomed into the household. Even after the death o Tina's father this warm, closely-knit group provided that sense of family which was so completely lacking in Weston's own experience. He made an exquisite portrait of Tina's mother, revealing the dignity and inner strength of the woman. Tina's younger sister Yolanda had started to work for him as a receptionist in 1922, and so the intimacy extended even outside the household. This relationship with Tina's family was to continue into the later years.

2

1923/1926 Mexico: The Legend of Tina and Weston

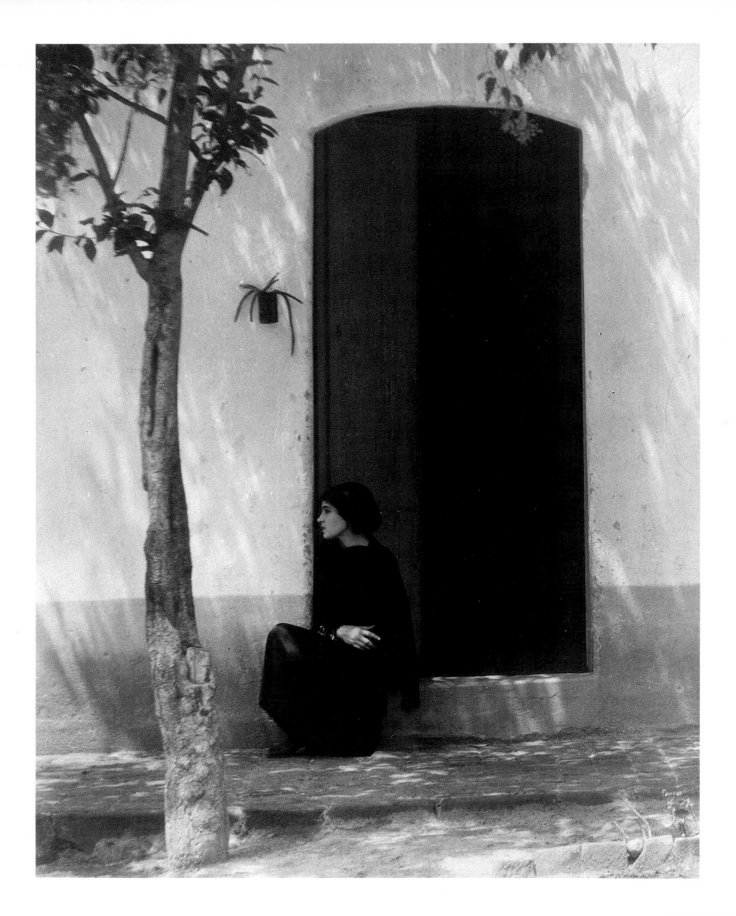

is not certain what brought about Weston's decision to leave wife and family and go off with Tina on what Ben Maddow calls a "psychic voyage." Was it perhaps a newfound confidence in himself and his work, gained from his trip to New York, as well as the warm reception of his work in Mexico? It may have been the fear of losing Tina when she left the United States for Mexico. Or it may have been the endless pressures of his family life in Glendale. Whatever combined to stimulate him into action, Tina, Edward, and his eldest son Chandler, then thirteen years old, left for Mexico on July 30, 1923, on board the S.S. Colima. They left "after months of preparation, after such endless delays that the proposed adventure seemed but a conceit of the imagination, never actually to materialize."[1] On board, Weston's jealousy manifested itself. "Thanks to Tina — her beauty — though I might have wished it otherwise! El Capitan has favored us in many ways: the use of his deck, refreshing drinks in his cabin, his launch to carry us ashore."

Their first overland trips from the port city of Manzanillo and then by train to Colima and Guadalajara gave them glimpses of the beauty and sharp contrasts of the Mexican landscape. One thing pleased them — there were no questions either in hotels or apartments as to the personal relations of the travelers.

Finally they reached Mexico City and their first house in Tacubaya, a suburb about forty minutes' trolley ride from the city. Weston describes it in a daybook entry (p. 15). "We have leased an old and beautiful hacienda for six months; ten rooms, each opening onto a spacious patio, 85 × 100, high ceilings and tall arched windows, barred, heavily shuttered, seeming to suggest possible attack ... the brick walls of our casa are fifteen inches thick and plastered in and out ..." They both enjoyed shopping and bargaining in the rambling market; Tina's familiarity with the language (she spoke Spanish with an Italian lilt) made these occasions both profitable and enjoyable. They bargained for everything and bought the Indian wares and food, as well as the bizarre objects sold in the market place. From their roof they could see the snow-capped volcanoes, Ixtacihuatl and Popocatepetl, and even sometimes the spires of the cathedral in Mexico City.

Unlike many other Americans who came to "attend" a revolution or to study the Aztec and the Mayan, and who tended to befriend fashionable intellectuals, Weston and Tina associated with artists and revolutionists. From the beginning they were not without friends in Mexico. Tina had already met many artists and intellectuals through Gómez Robelo. She was eager for Edward to meet them and see their work, as well as to have them know Weston's photographs. They met the painters, the poets, the writers. Tina renewed her acquaintance with Xavier Guerrero, then a young painter working

61

Next page:
Tina and Weston: their "anniversary" photographs,
Mexico, 1924
Collection: Zohmah Charlot, Honolulu

*Although originally attributed to Modotti, two
sources indicate that the photograph of Guerrero
is by Weston rather than by Tina. The date
however is uncertain. Weston did not arrive in
Mexico until August 1923. If the photograph was
made in Los Angeles when Guerrero was there it
would be the early part of 1923 or a later date,
prior to Weston's departure from Mexico.*

with Diego Rivera; his sister Elisa; Jean Charlot, the painter and writer who
had been in Mexico since 1921; José Vasconcelos, the guiding spirit behind th
painted walls; and the poet Juan de la Cabada. She had originally met
Guerrero in 1923, when he brought a folk art exhibition to Los Angeles. We ca
see the majesty and beauty of that man in one of Weston's great photographs.
They were to share a long and deep relationship after Weston left Mexico and
up until Guerrero left for the Soviet Union in 1928.

Unfortunately the stay in Tacubaya was very short-lived. They were obliged to
move because no telephone service was available in the outlying districts
and a telephone seemed essential to their livelihood. After much house-huntin
(little could compare to the charm of their hacienda), they found a house on
Calle Lucerna in the Colonia Juárez. This location gave them more opportunities
to explore Mexico City.

There was furious activity in the city in that year. The streets were full of
tramcars and *camiones* rushing about; vendors of *pulque*, sweets, fruits and
foods, toys and lacquerware were offering their wares. And music — *mariachi*
bands on the streets singing for themselves and for the revolution amid the
flower vendors offering their almost overpowering fragrances for *centavos*. The
acrid smoke of cooking fires mingled with pungent spices. The *Zócalo*
(Plaza) was dominated by the Mexican Cathedral, that imposing mixture of
architectural styles ranging from that of the Spanish *conquistadores* to
the baroque. Across a broad open expanse was the National Palace and other
public buildings. The *Zócalo* was also the scene of other kinds of activity.
Within the buildings, artists were at work in overalls just like the masons who
were working with them (at the same wage scale). Mexicans were arriving in
groups to petition for their rights, to ask for schools, or water for the pueblos,
or simply to observe and enjoy their capital and their heritage.

This activity extended to areas outside the city. Teachers were carrying books
from door to door; art became so popular that open-air art schools for children
were founded; painters were telling the story of Mexico and archaeologists and
anthropologists were digging the great ruined pyramids and temples to discov
the past, so that the Indian and the *mestizo* could take their proper place as th
foundation for the modern society.

A day's outing took Tina and Weston to Xochimilco, filled with asphalt
and stone roads leading to floating islands of flowers and vegetables and slender
willows divided by canals. All this reminded Tina of Italy, as did the sunshin
the colors, the gaiety of the people. They went to bullfights (to the pageantry
of which only Weston responded) and on other excursions into the countryside
participating in the local fiestas to which they were constantly invited.

On the occasion of Weston's first exhibition at "Aztec Land," a tourist shop in the center of the city, Diego Rivera together with his wife Guadalupe, responded to Weston's work with "a quiet, keen enjoyment." Thus began a long, not quite smooth friendship, with Diego and Lupe visiting Calle Lucerna and Weston and Tina joining the festivities at the Rivera household. Lupe was mercurial in her reactions to Tina — sometimes accusing Diego of having an affair with Tina, and at times penitent for her suspicions about Tina. She was never to believe that nothing existed between them. As recently as December 1971, in a newspaper interview in *Excelsior,* she said, "Diego was not a womanizer, but the women followed him very much. He began to visit a young Italian, and although he denied that they were having an affair, I did not believe him, and our situation was becoming more and more difficult; finally one day, he confessed that it was true; that he was having an affair with Modotti." Diego himself had said that it was in part his friendship with Tina which helped move Lupe toward a divorce.[2]

The parties which Tina and Weston had in their home became weekly reunions with much gaiety, singing, dancing, food and drink. Federico Marín (Lupe's younger brother) and Carlos and María Orozco Romero (he the painter and she the sister of Lupe) tell of one occasion when they were all together and Tina had prepared an excellent spaghetti with butter and cheese — the Neapolitan way. Federico describes Tina as "a mysterious beauty, without any vulgarity, very polite and introverted. She was always taking care of everything and spreading happiness all around her." An inquiry as to whether she was a merry person brought this response from him: "No — austere — terribly austere; not melancholic, neither sad nor tragic. Many men fell in love with her, they even committed suicide, but it wasn't her fault." Carlos Orozco Romero confirmed this and María remembers her as "a real woman — it's the only thing I can say because she was good in the home and good at her artistic activities."

It seems evident (at least from the Daybooks) that both Tina and Weston enjoyed other loves during this period in Mexico. Tina was characterized by some as a femme fatale and dangerous for men. Like so many beautiful women she had enormous sexual attraction for many men who desired her (an aspiring artist, rebuffed, once said that he wished Tina would kill him), but the nature of her relationship to several of those whose friendships she valued was unique. They were not casual infidelities. They were not simply the satisfactions of ego, of sex, or the expression of revenge and jealousy over Weston's sexual forays. That he resented her affairs is known, and he had said "Next time I'll pick a mistress ugly as hell." He had indicated in his Daybook (p. 58), "There is a certain inevitable sadness in the life of a much-sought-for beautiful woman, one like Tina especially, who, not caring sufficiently for associates among her own sex, craves comraderie and friendship from men as

ell as sex love..." He certainly sounds as though he resents Tina for her
ursuit of separate friendships – with or without sexual love – and it seems that
e underestimated her ability to give and receive friendship among the women
e knew. Anita Brenner tells of this period:

*e met sometime in 1923. In the weekly gatherings we were groups of painters
d writers. We were all eventually close friends; we were sort of looking for the
me things, working in the same channels. And it was not like the social
endships of now; it was a revolutionary atmosphere, almost like a workshop
mosphere, so we could all get into each other's "thing." I liked Tina very much;
e was very warm and basically a very gentle person. Very romantic and, in a
1y, clearer about where she was going (although she didn't know for sure) than
eston.*

hen asked about the rumors that Tina was considered promiscuous, Anita
renner answered quite emphatically:

*o! It was a romantic time in a way and it was a time of cutting loose and of
aking over the whole artistic world, the European breakthroughs, the world
eakthroughs and the Mexican breakthroughs were coming at the same time.
na was not a conventional person; she lived with Weston, but it was the same
marriage. There were the same relationships of caring and working together.
ue did have other lovers from time to time which I think Weston knew about,
it I think he did the same thing.*

is not difficult to assume that Tina, like so many women at that time, was
aking clear her disdain of bourgeois morality and affirming a single standard
 her relationships. Anita Brenner continues:
*asically she was an artist, and she was learning to photograph from Weston
hen I first met her. She was doing work in his darkroom and helping to finish
s work.*

na was starting to work on her own, and in Brenner's opinion what she did
as in an entirely different mood. "It was much softer and more
motional – Weston was working towards sharpness and an architectural feeling
d texture. Tina had a feeling for people and for all the romantic things that
ould come out of an Italian background."

na and Weston visited museums and private collections which revealed to
em the quality and depth of the ancient Mexican civilizations. They could
nderstand so much better the work of the artists filling Mexican walls with
e Mexican past. They broadened their social group to include politicos and
her foreigners in Mexico. Among the latter group were some Americans –
arleton Beals, writer and critic, Ella and Bertram Wolfe, then both teachers.
hey traveled to Tepotzotlán where the baroque architecture, rolling hills

Unidentified portrait, by Tina Modotti, 1925
Collection: Archivo Fotográfico Histórico,
Pachuca

Anita Brenner, Mexico, by Tina Modotti, 1925
Collection: Estate of Anita Brenner, Mexico

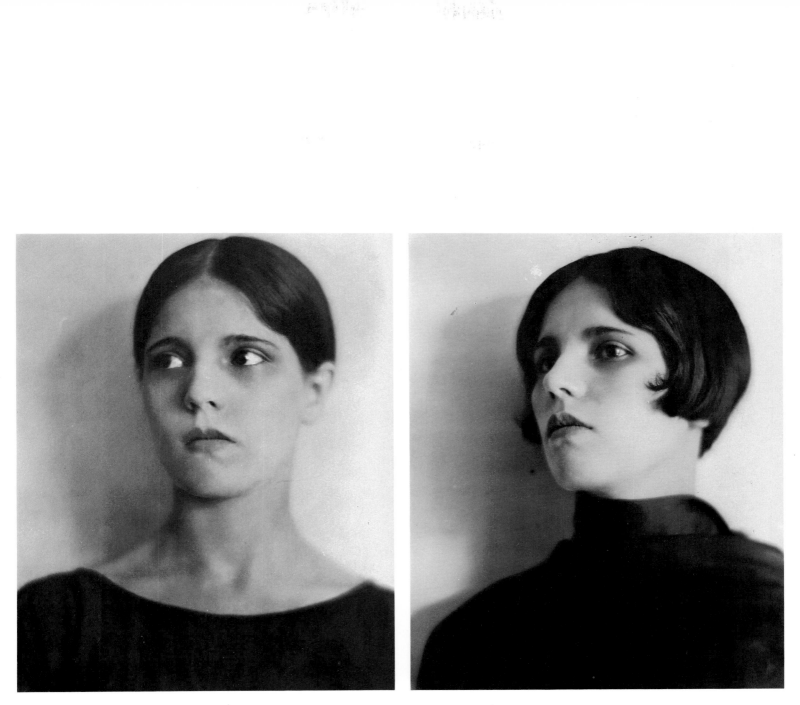

María Marín de Orozco, Mexico, by Tina Modotti, 1925

Edward Weston with his Graflex camera, Mexico,
by Tina Modotti, 1923
Collection: The Museum of Modern Art, New York

Opposite page:
Xavier Guerrero, Mexico, by Edward Weston, 1923—26
Collection: Charlot Collection, University of Hawaii at Manoa

and the maguey enchanted them and where they both took photographs. Tina made her most interesting abstraction of the tower of Tepotzotlán (see p. 109). "She is very happy over it and well she may be. I myself would be pleased to have done it," Weston had stated.

The distractions of their social life, their separate affairs and their work kept them somewhat apart. By the end of January 1924 Weston wrote: "The night before we had been alone — so seldom it happens now. She called me to her room and our lips met for the first time since New Year's Eve. Then the doorbell rang — Chandler and a friend — our mood was gone." Yet they found time to sit together on their roof (azotea), reading aloud, discussing books, Tina recalling memories of Italy. And talking about their own love, which Tina expressed so beautifully on Weston's birthday in a letter, "a note of two words and three purple hyacinth buds" which conveyed more in simple emotion than pages could have done. The only words were: "Edward, Edward!" A single cry of many emotions: love, passion, anguish, tenderness.

Tina was able to make all kinds of lasting friendships, among them with Pablo O'Higgins, an American painter born in San Francisco, who had come to Mexico in 1924 and become an assistant to Rivera. O'Higgins has recalled the first time he met Tina:

I think it was one of the moments when Tina came to the Secretaría de Educación *to take photographs, because Diego was very interested in Tina's photographing the work in progress so that you would see a piece of detail and the drawing on the plaster — to see at the base of things, as Diego called it. That's where I first saw Tina. Naturally, I was just another person, but she impressed me immediately as a beautiful woman. I mean beautiful — not trying to be beautiful — but born beautiful. Very much of Tina was always like that — never pretending to be anything she wasn't. Very open and frank. I told her that I would like to see some of her work and she invited me to where they were staying . . . she was living with Weston on Calle Lucerna, and so when I went there to see Tina, I met Weston too. We talked of many things and the next time I went I made a sketch of Tina that I liked very much because I liked the way she was sitting.*

Rivera and Charlot also made fine drawings of Tina at this time (see pp. 74, 73).

By May of 1924 Tina and Weston had to move again, this time to Avenida Vera Cruz. One of the Mexican women who came to sit for Weston at this time has said, "I keep a very good souvenir of her (Tina's) charm and personality — she used blue gins [sic] that were very unusual for women at this time." They continued their exploration of Mexico City, roaming the old streets and njoying the bustling activity, visiting old, out-of-the-way churches. On one uch day they calmly ventured into a photographer's studio and announced hemselves as a wedded couple celebrating their first wedding anniversary. hey wanted a photograph to commemorate their anniversary. The postures and ackground were carefully planned by the photographer, while Tina and Veston obediently kept the pose and managed to strike a serious attitude (was all play-acting?) (see p. 63). It would appear that both were dressed in fairly onventional clothes. Tina, it seemed, always dressed as herself, not in a ostume arranged to fit her into a particular role. She was a small woman, and lmost always dressed in dark blue or black, preferably in skirts and blouses hen she did not wear the blue jeans. Of course, there were the Mardi Gras arties with funny masks and costumes, and Tina and Weston loved to change lothes on these occasions. Even with their exciting social life and their avels, Tina was to pose time and time again for Weston. Once she read poetry o that he could "attempt the registration of her remarkably mobile face in ction (see p. 87)."[3]

ina had been going off on her own using her camera to record the circus, uppet shows, churches, plazas, as well as the frescoes of Rivera. She worked 1 the darkroom on her own negatives, helping Weston with his, and also rinting from old negatives by unknown photographers for Anita Brenner's ook. She had her first public showing that year in the Palacio de Minerva, gether with Weston and other artists. Weston was to comment, "Tina's lose othing by comparison with mine — they are her own expression."[4]

omehow the political scene — whether in the informal discussions at their eekly reunions, the meetings they attended, or the activities of friends hose lives were completely devoted to the revolution — was always present in heir lives.

1 spite of Weston's repeated success with his work in Mexico, his concern and nxiety for his family back in Glendale caused him to leave Mexico after ighteen months of separation from his other boys. In December 1924 before e left, Tina wrote a note to him (out of respect for the other's privacy, they ften exchanged written messages within the household): "What is the use of ords between Edward and I? He knows me and I know him and we both have uith in each other. And that to me, Edward, seems the most precious gain e have acquired from each other — the faith in each other. I will be a good girl hile you are gone Edward — I will work hard and that for two reasons — that ou may be proud of me and that the time of our separation may move more wiftly. Edward — beloved — thank you — whatever comes." They spent hours efore his departure trying to reconcile their lives, and Tina claimed that her ind was clearly focused — "I want to go with you Edward, to be your

Drawing of Tina, by Pablo O'Higgins, 1924

Next page:
Drawing of Tina, by Jean Charlot, 1924

Following pages:
Drawing of Tina, by Diego Rivera, 1926

Virgin Earth *(above) and* Life and Earth *(below) by Diego Rivera,*
Panels in Chapel, Escuela Nacional de Agricultura,
Chapingo, Mexico, by Tina Modotti, 1925

Para Tina Modotti
Diego Rivera . 26

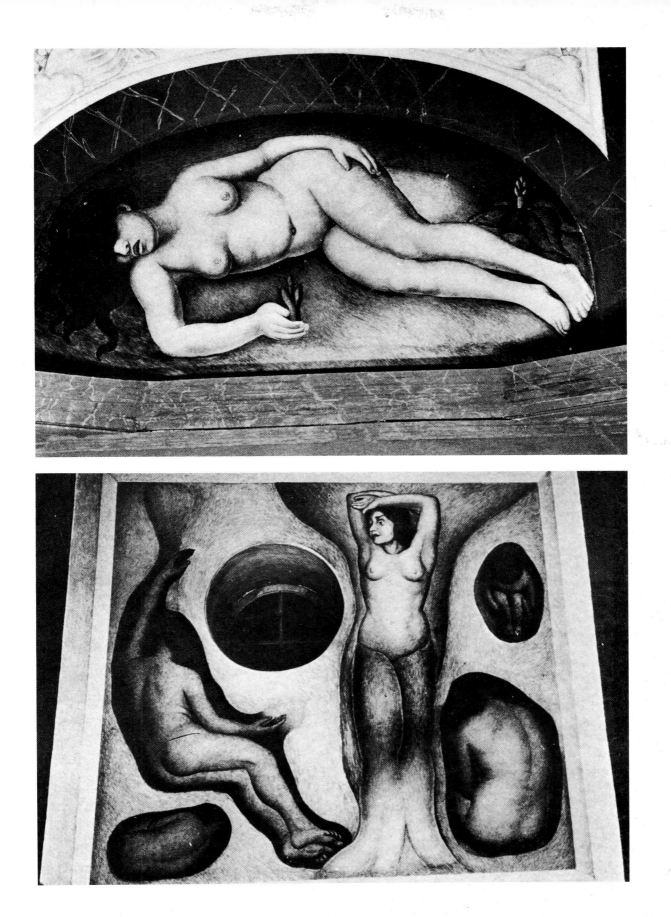

'apprentice' and work in photography." Chandler, on the other hand, wanted to remain and Tina had offered to care for him but he left with his father at the end of December 1924.

Weston was to return to Mexico but Tina wrote him frequently, often confessing (July 7, 1925): "I have not been very 'creative,' Edward — less than a print a month — that is terrible! And yet it is not lack of interest so much as lack of discipline and power of execution...speaking of my personal self — I cannot — as you once proposed to me — solve the problem of life by losing myself in the problem of art — not only I cannot do that but I even feel that the problem of life hinders my problem of art."

Here perhaps are the first stirrings of realizations of the incompatibility of her life and her art: to be with Weston, and to be his apprentice, conflicted with her growing consciousness in the atmosphere of social responsibility. We must remember that Tina, born in Italy and raised in poverty, was strongly influenced by the views of her proletarian father. At this time the memories of her youth must have been reawakened by her surroundings, providing still another link in her own development and producing a strong kinship with the Mexican people and their problems. We can also assume that the ambience in Los Angeles with Robo's family was entirely bourgeois. Certainly Weston and the group which met in Robo's studio were, in effect, bourgeois-turned-bohemian-and-radical (though not politically), Tina being probably the only true proletarian among them. At the same time, she was posing for Diego Rivera's murals in the Chapel at the Chapingo Agricultural School, "Virgin Earth" and "Life and Earth." These daily contacts brought her into the company of a dedicated political person who, while not consciously proselytizing, must have expressed his views to her and educated her about another way of life.

Weston was at this time not simply apolitical but outspokenly anti-Communist. In their personal relationship he held out little hope for their lives together. One wonders if they ever discussed the possibilities of his divorce from Flora and their eventual marriage, or if there was some unspoken understanding that this was impossible.

Tina was still on a search for her own identity. She was certainly aware of the conflicts within her, but her personal independence and instinctive identification with political struggle was not to be resolved until she made personal commitments to a politically active role. And also, with Weston gone, she may have yearned for another emotional involvement in her life which would help point the way to some clarification of the future.
In August 1925 after an absence of eight months, Weston returned to Mexico.

This time he was accompanied by his second eldest son, fourteen-year-old Brett. When they arrived in Guadalajara, Tina and Elisa Guerrero, sister to Xavier, were at the station platform to meet them. They spent ten days here, during which time Weston's and Tina's work was shown in Guadalajara's *Museo del Estado*. They had happy reunions with the Marín family, whose home was always open to them. Returning to Mexico City, their lives resumed the old pattern: parties, dances, excursions, sittings, visits from Tina's sister Mercedes, John Dewey, René d'Harnoncourt. Life in the household went on as before until it was interrupted by Tina's departure for San Francisco to visit her mother, who was seriously ill. Weston noted that "the house seemed so strangely empty." He appears to have been ambivalent in his feelings toward Tina at this time, resenting her lovers, though he doesn't name any one specifically except for a Dr. M. who just wanted to worship her. At the same time he felt no pressure in Tina's love for him since there was never any indication of the possessiveness of "a woman madly in love." And he freely "romped" with the servants in the household and pursued Xavier's sister at the same time.

In San Francisco on January 25 Tina wrote:

Eduardito, a letter from you today. How I look forward to those long, cream-colored envelopes. When one is handed to me a thrill goes over my whole body. Things have been very chaotic and difficult with me but Consuelo [Kanaga — a photographer friend from Mexico] has done much to help me. Today Dan took me all around to camera dealers in search of a second-hand Graflex and trying to sell my Corona — dear little Corona — I feel so attached to it but you won't think me ungrateful for trying to sell it? I explained in my last letter the reason and I can't get one without selling the other. There is much I want to talk to you about — all my impressions of the U.S. all my reactions — all my ideas of working differently in photography when I return...little mamacita is feeling fine these days — oh, what a relief for us! We pet her and spoil her to death — her regards to you — she and everybody here also loves you — your name is always mentioned in connection with something nice...

In a letter she confides a feeling of helplessness:

When it comes to doing things for myself I just feel impotent — I don't know which way to start or turn — you know what they say about a prophet in one's own country. Well, in a way it works for me too — you see — this might be called my home town — well, of all the friends and acquaintances not one takes me seriously as a photographer — not one has asked me to show my work — only the ones I met through you...I am going to work hard when I return to Mexico and differently — if I can get a Graflex — I have always been too restrained in my work as you well know but I feel now with a Graflex I will be

Opposite page:
Federico Marín, Jean Charlot, Tina Modotti on the azotea, by Edward Weston, 1924

Tina (fourth from the left) and Weston (third on the right) in the Marín family home, Guadalajara, Mexico, 1924

Chandler Weston, María Marín de Orozco, Diego Rivera, Tina Modotti and Lupe Rivera on an outing in Xochimilco, Mexico D.F.

Federico Marín, Mexico, by Tina Modotti, 1924

able to loosen up...*This is all for now dear, short but hardly sweet because I fe rather gloomy... but it is only temporary so — don't worry — rather forgive me — seems so long, so long since I have been near you and talked with you — I miss you dear...*

Imogen Cunningham, a friend of Weston's, had met Tina on the occasion of her visit to San Francisco. She and her then-husband Roi Partridge purchased the photograph of the wine glasses. Cunningham recalls, "to me she was a performer of real interest... I was never critical of her, never noticed her accent if she had one, just took in her beauty."

Tina's feelings of impotence and helplessness at this time may be an expressic of feeling alien in the ambience of the United States where indeed she was less at home than in Mexico in the household she shared with Weston. It is no surprising that she felt that Mexico was "home" (this in spite of the seeming frivolity of Weston's and her separate sexual encounters). She could communicate with him, with her close friends, and share with them the seriousness of their professional and social concerns in light of the political climate there.

These were perilous days in Mexico. Plutarco Elías Calles, a member of the Obregón cabinet, had been President since the end of 1924. He had stron support from Luis Morones, a labor boss with a tight political machine, who had become his Minister of Labor, thus allowing Calles to proclaim his a labo government. The Federation of Unions, known as CROM — the Revolutionary Federation of Mexican Labor — worked hand in hand with the government; almost all other unions outside of CROM were broken. There seemed to be some progress: roads were built, a series of dams, schools and hospitals; there was a business boom but with little more than lip service to the demands of th revolution. While work on the new constitution continued, it produced little against the oil interests and the power of the church; land distribution programs had slowed down to a halt. The Church conflict grew with a decree that the priesthood would be under government control. The Church denounced the decree and supported guerrillas called *Cristeros*, who spread propaganda, raided the rural schools and murdered the teachers.

At this time also relations were strained with the United States because of potential dangers to the oil and land interests and because of Mexico's suppor of the Nicaraguan resistance to the U.S. Marines. Tina had worked with the Hands-off Nicaragua Committee in Mexico (see p. 150).

In March of 1926, Tina and Weston again exhibited together, billed as "The Emperor of Photography — the *bellísima* Tina Modotti — an irresistible

The commission to investigate Mexican art was given to Anita Brenner by the former Rector of the Universidad Autónoma de Mexico, Dr. Alfonso Pruneda.

combination." This reference to Tina as "the beautiful Tina Modotti" surely displeased her. Therefore the review of the exhibition by Diego Rivera must have struck a welcome note: "Tina Modotti has done marvels in sensibility on a plane, perhaps more abstract, more aerial, even more intellectual, as is natural for an Italian temperament. Her work flowers perfectly in Mexico and harmonizes with our passion."[5]

They continued their excursions out of the capital and both were excited by Anita Brenner's proposal for a project to record the art, architecture and crafts of Mexico. They went off to Puebla, Oaxaca, Michoacán, Jalisco, Guanajuato and Querétaro. Brenner was writing her now famous book *Idols Behind Altars* for which Weston and Tina had already made the photographs, and had in mind a further exploration of the past of Mexico through its art. These archives are in the estate of Anita Brenner, Mexico.

Yolanda Modotti, Tina's sister, San Francisco, by Tina Modotti, 1925

Often Tina worked alone and sometimes together with Weston in recording the works. Given the unsettled times, they were happy to leave Mexico City and the uneasiness there. Many of their friends were now scattered. In Michoacán they learned with horror of the death of their great friend, Manuel Hernández Galvan, then a senator who was killed by political opponents. They were concerned about the fate of their other friends. They were becoming weary of travel week after week in areas where the rainy season inhibited work and made living uncomfortable. They kept seeing posters of the now-dead Galván as they moved into new towns. Finally they returned to Mexico City at least satisfied with the work accomplished.

But the home they shared in Mexico had changed. There were still visitors streaming in and out, and they all went to parties with their friends. But the legend of Tina and Edward was on the wane. Each was pursuing a different path. Weston was trying to have an affair with a woman he identified only as M., and Tina may already have begun her involvement with Xavier Guerrero. This was no ordinary rift, not just the cooling of fervor: Weston was finished with Mexico and impatient to be reunited with his other sons. Brett, who was beginning to produce photographs which delighted Weston, also was eager to return to the United States. In November they left, and Weston wrote in his Daybook: "The leaving of Mexico will be remembered for the leaving of Tina. The barrier between us was for the moment broken. Not till we were on the Paseo in a taxi rushing for the train did I allow myself to see her eyes. But when I did and saw what they had to say, I took her to me...Tina with tear-filled eyes. This time, Mexico, it must be adios forever. And you, Tina? I feel it must be farewell forever too."

Were Tina's tear-filled eyes a sign of bleak despair as another phase in her life

ad ended? There appears to have been no discussion about the possibility
of Tina's leaving with Weston. Tina had made her decision to remain in
Mexico, to pursue her own life and work there. She also at this time appears to
have had firm convictions about her revolutionary feminism, which did not
wait to be liberated but which she pursued in every aspect of her life.
Remarriage — to Weston or anyone else — was of no interest to her.

The relationships that Tina shared with women contradict still another myth
that even Weston helped to create: that Tina, like many beautiful women,
did not care sufficiently for associates among her own sex. The words of Anita
Brenner, María Marín de Orozco (Lupe Rivera's sister) and Emily Edwards
seem to indicate a warm response to her.

Pablo O'Higgins had introduced Emily Edwards to Tina in 1926 shortly before
Weston and Brett were to leave Mexico. Miss Edwards recalls:

*At that time, Tina, Edward Weston and his young son were together in Mexico
City. I remember seeing a series of photos of her head, taken while she was
talking; the tragedy she expressed astonished me. Tina always seemed to be the
same person; whether as woman, artist or revolutionist — all-of-a-piece, as she
lived simply what she was. Basically, she was beautiful. Her studio was always
in simple good order, and this easy efficiency was in whatever she was doing. I
was outside her revolutionary activities, but attended one meeting where she was
in charge; and quiet efficiency ruled.*
*Tina was naturally generous and sensitive to others, but she did not tolerate
intrusion nor was she unaware of the failings of her friends. Certainly she was
unconventional, but she was shocked by vulgarity and presumption. She
has her friendships of convenience but knew what she was doing. Tina had
many different kinds of friends. I was deeply in her debt for generous friendship
and as you can see I both loved and trusted her.*

Although she never had a child, Tina nevertheless had great affinity with
young people. We can feel her response to the children of Mexico in her
photographs, and sense her emotions in what she captured in their expressive
eyes. She had, after all, cared for the younger children in her own family,
who also had been hungry and sad. She had spent a good deal of time under
the same roof with Chandler first, then Brett, and felt deeply for Weston's boys
and his relationship with them. The Sunday morning after their departure, she
was to write:

*Edward; I woke up with the nice feeling that you were here — My first thought
was, I wonder if Edward is up yet? — but the illusion did not last long — and the
vision of your and Brett's empty rooms hurt me as much as yesterday after my
return here — I want to write you at length Edward — but not now — I cannot see
now —*

*Benvenuto Modotti, Tina's brother, San Francisco,
by Tina Modotti, 1925*

81

Above and next page:
Tina, Mexico, by Edward Weston, 1925
Collection: Center for Creative Photography, Tucson, Arizona

Tina, Mexico, by Edward Weston, 1925
Collection: Center for Creative Photography, Tucson, Arizona

Next page:
Tina on the azotea, Mexico, by Edward Weston, 1924
Collection: Center for Creative Photography, Tucson, Arizona

85

Tina, Mexico, by Edward Weston, 1925
Collection: Center for Creative Photography, Tucson, Arizona

Opposite page:
Tina on the azotea, Mexico, by Edward Weston, c. 1924
Collection: Center for Creative Photography, Tucson, Arizona

*Modern American and British Poetry, *edited*
by Louis Untermeyer, has Pound's Canto LXXXI*
on p. 172. It begins:
What thou lovest well remains,
The rest is dross
What thou lov'st well shall not be reft from thee
What thou lov'st well is thy true heritage
Whose world, or mine or theirs,
or is it of none?

You know that poem of Ezra Pound on page 172 — You are that to me
Edward — No matter what others mean to me you are that — only you were
embittered and had lost faith in me — but I never did because I respect
the manifold possibilities of being found in all of us and also because I accept
the tragic conflict between life which continually changes and form which
fixes it immutable —
But I cannot write more — this terrible gnawing at my heart won't let me. Till
soon dear — you are on the train now but when this reaches you, you will
be surrounded by all your boys — I keep visualizing the picture of you with
your boys for it brings a smile of great tenderness and peace on my lips —*

The legend of Tina and Weston was over. She had now come to another
crisis — another turning point in her life. She was thirty years old, once
married, she had experienced the death of a husband and father, she had
physically and spiritually left the United States (had she ever felt a kinship
with it?), she had had three years of a relationship which seemingly had been
fulfilling in all its aspects. By all accounts Tina was an honest person, honest
in her relationship and honest to herself. Weston's departure was not
precipitous, nor did their separation come as a surprise to her. It was
probably not bleak despair that caused her tear-filled eyes but the realization
that, whatever her passionate attachment to Weston had been, that aspect of
their relationship was over. In all probability she had already become deeply
involved with Xavier Guerrero. Her fundamental independence could be seen
in her own view of the world, and in her future, which of necessity was also the
rupture with Weston.

"The tragic conflict between life which continually changes and form which
fixes it immutable" was probably the recognition deep within herself that
the barrier between Weston and herself was unbridgeable. Each had to go along
consciously chosen paths, separate though they might be. And Tina must have
cherished what remained for them to share — a rare and close communication.

There is a special tone in Tina's letters to Weston from this time onward.
She never admonishes him for having abandoned her and their life in Mexico,
but continually expresses a warmth and depth of friendship shared. Weston
too in retrospect recognized what he called "the fineness of our association,"
and this quality surely made possible their closeness through letters.

3

26/1930 Mexico: Commitment to Revolution, Expulsion

Tina found her way into the life stream of Mexico. Passionate woman that she was, she poured her emotions into politics, identifying herself with Mexico's struggles and aspirations. From this point onward it was not difficult for her to align herself with Guerrero and with the Communist cause.

Xavier and Tina had met briefly in Los Angeles in 1923 and resumed their acquaintance on her arrival in Mexico. He had been working with Siqueiros and Rivera on the newspaper *El Machete* since 1922 and had collaborated with Rivera on the frescoes in Chapingo. Although his art had involved him from youth with revolutionary Mexico, he became a political activist, living and working through the Communist Party in the service of world revolution. He undoubtedly saw a good deal of Tina during the period when Weston was in Mexico, and perhaps even before Weston's departure the relationship between Tina and Xavier had developed into more than friendship. This might have provided a sense of security at this point of Tina's life, not out of a sense of loneliness after the final break with Weston, but more through a sense of identification with a cause. She became a member of the Communist Party in 1927. She and Xavier, as artists, were able to share the same aesthetic concerns as well as their own place in the revolutionary struggle.

It has been suggested that Tina's association with the artists made her turn to Communism. Surely it contributed to her formalizing her position at this time, but we must also remember her early childhood sufferings and deprivations. Her own experiences in factories were still deep in her consciousness.

The photographs which Tina and Weston made in Mexico show very clearly the differences in their response to Mexico. Weston's truth is most visible in the individuals to whom he responded and whose portraits are revelations of sitter and photographer, particularly those he made of Tina, Diego Rivera, Lupe Marín, D. H. Lawrence. "He felt strongly the impact of the face itself, the head as a sculptured object, within which the springs of hate and love continually wound and unwound . . . an explosion of character itself."[1] Tina's photographs show a development of her style in relation to what was at the center of her being: the ordinary people she had observed, the tools, the burdens of life exalting her chosen subjects with a touch of poetry. She was able to make visible the humility, simplicity, solitude and fortitude of the Mexican people. She communicated her feelings about them with a poignancy that is unforgettable. Tina had a quiet comprehension of all suffering.

It is apparent from available letters that Tina wrote relatively little about her own work to Weston. Occasionally she would send him a print of one of her favorites, like the Calla lily (see p. 116). She hardly ever wrote all the details of her deepening political involvements, although she did write enough to

Opposite page:
Corn, Guitar, Cartridge, by Tina Modotti, 1928
Collection: Comitato Tina Modotti, Trieste

indicate her commitments and those of their mutual friends. She remained devoted to Weston's development as an artist, bringing his new work to the attention of people whose opinion both of them cared about. She would report these faithfully to him.

Tina also ardently expressed her own reactions to his work, and those reaction continued to be of importance to Weston. She remarks in one very important letter: "My God, Edward, your last photographs surely took my breath away. feel speechless in front of them..." (July 25, 1927). She continues: *Edward — nothing before in art has affected me like these photographs — I just cannot look at them a long while without feeling exceedingly perturbed — they disturb me not only mentally, but physically — there is something so pure and a the same time so perverse about them — they contain both the innocence of natural things and the morbidity of a sophisticated, distorted mind — They mak me think of lilies and of embryos at the same time — they are mystical and eroti*

She was referring to the series of shell photographs which Weston started to d in June 1927 which were astonishing revelations of the purity and monumentality of natural forms, work truly unlike anything ever done in photography before. Although not all of Tina's letters to Weston were consulted, and his to her have vanished, we can assume a steady exchange of correspondence. Their letters appear to have been numbered, so that if one number did not appear they would be aware of even the slightest discontinuity in their communication.

In 1927 Tina was to meet a man deeply involved in the political struggle of th times who was later to become her political mentor and, in the thirties, her companion. He was also an Italian; he came from Trieste, an area very much like that of Udine. A committed anti-Fascist, he had known years of revolutionary activity in Italy as well as in the United States. It was perhaps this man, Vittorio Vidali, who rekindled in Tina the consciousness of her Italian heritage and the passion to return to Italy. He, like other radicals and liberals, had rallied to the defense of Nicola Sacco, a shoe-factory worker, an Bartolomeo Vanzetti, a fish peddler, who were convicted in 1921 of the murde of a Massachusetts paymaster and his guard.

The United States from the middle of the twenties onward was affected by hysterical mistrust of atheists, anarchists, aliens, socialists and liberals in the trade union movements. Both Sacco and Vanzetti were anarchists, both were aliens who had evaded the army draft. Neither had a criminal record, nor did they have any of the money which was supposed to have been stolen from the paymaster. They were tried in the summer of 1921, convicted, and sentenced death. From that time, Sacco and Vanzetti became the cause of liberals and dicals. Poets responded to the gentleness of the two humble Italians who were guilty only of a deep sincerity in their anarchistic political philosophy; painters were deeply moved by the contrast between the strength and integrity of the prisoners and the self-righteousness of the prosecution and their relentless pursuit of the mock trial. Protest meetings were held all over the United States, in Europe, and throughout Latin America. Just two months before Sacco and Vanzetti were to be electrocuted in 1927 Vittorio Vidali was deported from the United States and went to Mexico. He attended an important demonstration in June of that year for Sacco and Vanzetti. It was there that he first met Tina Modotti. Vidali was a challenging combination of physical and intellectual strength. He was a monolithic composition in which all of the pieces fell together: a gravelly voice which spoke brilliantly and, at moments, pedagogically; not a tall man, but with bulk that was hard, strong, and unyielding; he possessed a security within and a mastery of Marxist ideology. His intellect is broadly acknowledged; his warmth and charm recognized by those who knew him. Although Tina had been working more concretely in the militant revolutionary movement since Weston's departure, she now aligned herself with the Anti-Imperialist League of the Americas. She had participated in the Hands-off Nicaragua Campaign established in Mexico City, and helped found the first anti-Fascist Italian committee there. That same year she had become a member of the Communist party. Tina's emotional involvement with Vittorio Vidali was not to take place for several years. In part, a passionate devotion to the Communist cause and to the anti-Fascist movement motivated their friendship. Vidali also brought to their relationship an intellectual and spiritual strength which served Tina's needs at that time.

Her letters to Weston continued, although her communication with him was on a different level. In July 1927 she reported on a visit to a school; her observations, in view of the political difficulties of the time, are worth noting: *Some people — friends of Ella [Wolfe] here from New York — they wanted to visit the school in* Colonia de la Bolsa. *Since I was also anxious to know it I offered to take them — Edward when we left the place we all had tears in our eyes — What that Sr. Oropeza (the founder and director) has accomplished is something I will not attempt here to relate — And when we complimented him on his achievement he answered, "I could have done nothing without the children!" They have departments of Carpentering — Baking — Sewing — Printing — Photography — Farming — Shoemaking, etc. Everything on the smallest scale is certain but serious — each department has an expert person as a teacher — I mean a regular professional baker, shoemaker, etc. Everything is run on the basis of syndicates — every department has its delegate — they hold weekly meetings and discuss the problems arising during the week and the way to improve everything. They have a department of justice also elected by the boys and formed by the boys — One case is this: a boy was found stealing a*

considerable amount of money from the general funds — how do you suppose the
punished the boy? By making him their treasurer —
Besides manual labor they all have certain hours for general instruction — and
some for gymnasium, games, etc. I would write on and on about this but I
would after all not be able to at all — Sr. Oropeza is writing a book on the
founding and developing of the school — John Dewey (one of his greatest
admirers) promised to finance the publication —
I am indeed sorry that we never visited the school while you were here as we ha
so often planned — Dear one — this is all for tonight —

Tina still enjoyed communicating her news, thoughts about Mexico and
their mutual friends to Weston. She continued her travels, her photography,
was devoting more of her time to serious pursuits and not living the
life of an expatriate. Given the reputation which Tina gained as a promiscuou:
tempting woman, her behavior seems extraordinarily different from some
American expatriates whose lives in other parts of the world were devoted to
creativeness of a sort, wastefulness and phoniness in their defiance of the
bourgeois world. But Tina's life was inner-directed; she was neither indiscreet
nor indiscriminate, she was possessed of a discipline, a drive and a capacity
respond to the life around her. She was also involved with a man who shared
these qualities.

Weston's photograph reveals so much of Xavier Guerrero. Dominant in the
beautifully carved face is the sense of mystery, of power, of all of Mexico's
pride, of *Indianismo* which seems to be impenetrable.

What dominated each of them at this time seems to have been their
consciousness of a human struggle that was greater than their own private
involvement. Xavier was later to leave Mexico for the Soviet Union, where he
remained for some years in the Lenin school in Moscow. We do not know
whether it was Tina's intention to join him there, but they remained in close
touch through letters, and Tina kept him apprised of events in Mexico by her
own reporting and through periodicals she sent him. She was going through
another momentous change in her life; she was living alone and eagerly
embracing the new paths her life was taking, broadening the scope of her wor
in photography and political involvements. She had time as well for old and
new friends. The renowned Mexican photographer Manuel Alvarez Bravo tells
us what he found in Tina:
I met her for the first time in 1927. I was in Oaxaca where I worked during the
years 1925—26. While in Oaxaca I received many magazines and other
publications from Mexico City, and through them I learned about Tina Modott
particularly through two magazines — one published by Gabriel Figueroa
and Gabriel Fernández Ledesma, who was also her friend, and Frances Toor's

magazine, Mexican Folkways. *I had been working in photography since 1924 and was very eager to meet her. In 1927 she had that same elegance and grace she had brought with her to Mexico. The walls of her studio were white and clean; later she started to write some of Lenin's and Marx's phrases on them. Even before that time on a visit to Mexico City I had seen an exhibition of Weston's photographs and of course there were also some of Tina's — this was during 1924 or 1925 — they were in the romantic period (she had two periods — the romantic and the revolutionary). One day a friend pointed out two people, Tina and Weston; each was carrying a camera. That was the first time I saw her, near La Santísima Church. They looked at the church but didn't take any pictures. That was my first glimpse of Tina, but I really met her in 1927...I visited her on many occasions and she was generally very busy — meetings with people like Carleton Beals and Frances Toor but they were speaking English and I don't know how to speak English. But very often on a visit she would show me what she had done and what Weston was sending her and we would talk for a long while...At the meetings she conducted herself very gracefully and in fund-raising she would speak in Spanish and in Italian.*

Tina was not only sympathetic to Manuel as an individual but was equally impressed with his work and unselfishly encouraged the development of his art. She sent some of his prints to Weston without identifying them. Weston responded with a letter addressed to M. Alvarez Bravo, asking pardon since he was not sure whether he was addressing a *Señor, Señora,* or *Señorita.* He asked whether they had been sent for an exhibition in Germany for which he had been making a collection, or for his inspection. And his letter continued: *But no matter why I have them, I must tell you how much I am enjoying them. Sincerely, they are important — and if you are a new worker, photography is fortunate in having someone with your viewpoint. It is not often I am stimulated to enthusiasm over a group of photographs...I will not write more, until I hear from you — some explanation and word about yourself.*

Weston added this comment in his Daybook:
I have been the recipient of a package of photographs. Photographs of better than usual technique, and of excellent viewpoint...so many were of subject matter I might have chosen — rocks, juguetes, a skull, construction. I wonder if this person...does not know my work, or Tina's? In fact I had a suspicion — and still wonder — if these prints are not from Tina — under an assumed name — perhaps to get my unbiased opinion...it is all a very nice mystery.[2]

Tina's own work was being published; commendations and commissions were coming from all sides. She was happily earning a livelihood through photography and expressed her feeling about her work to Weston: "You don't know how often the thought comes to me of all I owe to you for having been *the*

In 1929, Weston met Richard Neutra, the important Austrian architect of the International Style who had moved to Los Angeles in 1925. Neutra had been asked to organize the American entries for the pivotal "Film and Foto" exhibition to be held by the Deutsche Werkbund in Stuttgart that year. Neutra asked Weston to take charge of selecting the American photographs for the show and to write a catalogue essay. Weston wrote to Hagemeyer in February for help, "I have much to discuss with you about this — too long to write down. But your work will be an important note — which I take for granted you will let me have."

"Have you given up thoughts of showing in Germany? Prints would have to be in my hands before I go south, that is, here (Carmel) by Thursday. Otherwise too late. Unmounted prints wanted. I seem to have fizzled on this show. Tina Modotti refuses to show old work and has no new. Margrethe (Mather) — no answer. Imogen (Cunningham) will send her flower forms. Brett (Weston) and E.W., each 20."

It is strange that there is no mention of the work of the great photographers working in Mexico during the early twenties: Hugo Brehme and Guillermo Kahlo, the father of Frida Kahlo. Alvarez Bravo reports that while Weston admired Brehme's technique he disliked his painterly approach, preferring straight photography.

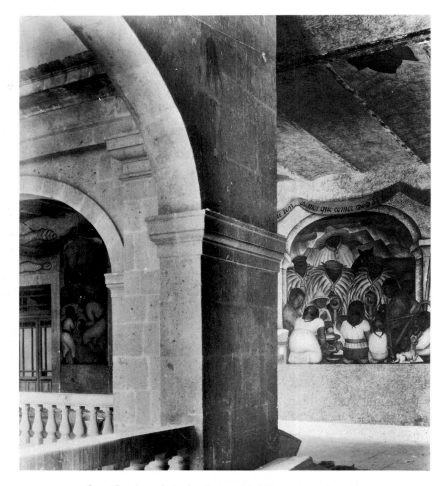

Corridor: Lunch in the Rain, *third floor, second patio,*
Secretaría de Educación Pública, Mexico, D.F.

Next page:
Detail of mural in the Secretaría de Educación by Diego Rivera
showing Tina, on the right, distributing arms to the people, 1923–28

José Clemente Orozco at work on his mural, by Tina Modotti
Collection: Instituto de Investigaciones Estéticas, Universidad Nacional
Autónoma, Mexico D.F.

Next page:
Architectural detail with murals by José Clemente
Orozco, Mexico, by Tina Modotti, 1923

St. Francis Helping the Poor, *by José Clemente Orozco,*
architectural detail, by Tina Modotti, 1923
Collection: Charlot Collection, University of Hawaii at Manoa

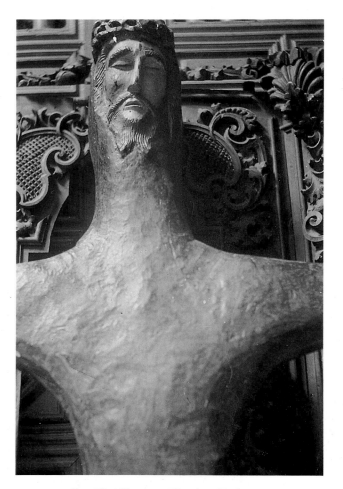

Crucifix, Museum, Morelia, Michoacan,
by Tina Modotti, 1925
Collection: Estate of Anita Brenner, Mexico

Head of Christ, by Tina Modotti, 1925
Collection: Estate of Anita Brenner, Mexico

Jean Charlot in the foreword to The Artist in New York by José Clemente Orozco, (University of Texas Press, Austin and London, 1974) states: "In many a letter Orozco stresses his pressing need for photographs of his murals, in the hope that American architects would give him the walls he had been denied at home. Tina Modotti and I attempted the task."

Orozco was quite clear in his instructions to Tina with regard to photographs. He was very aware of the architectural details and how his panels often echoed the architectural curves of the stone arches, the landing of the stairs. He often sent instructions together with small drawings and these directives posed many problems. "Easy to sketch from memory in his letters, Orozco's photographic directives posed substantial problems when weighed in situ. For days we worked throughout the daylight hours, stopping only for a beer and sandwich brought by Tina's friend Julio Antonio Mella."

In a letter from Charlot to the author he stated: "She was in her own right a sensitive artist, and her photographs of white-washed adobe walls will be rediscovered in time as precursors of the minimalists. She was a selfless person. Having joined the Communist Party, she gently complained that comrades, knowing her to be by trade a photographer, expected their family portraits free of charge. In her help to artists, she was untiring."

one important being, at a certain time of my life, and when I did not know which way to turn, the one and only vital guidance and influence that initiate me in this work that is not only a means of livelihood but a work that I have come to love with real passion and that offers such possibilities of expression (even though lately I am not making full use of these possibilities)."

At this time Tina was occupied with assignments from *Mexican Folkways* and with photographing the frescoes of Rivera, Guerrero, Máximo Pacheco and Jos Clemente Orozco. Orozco, who was then in New York, commissioned Tina to photograph particular sections of his frescoes, directing her as to the position of the camera in relation to his work. He communicated these instructions to Jean Charlot, and Tina would try to fulfill his wishes. "Tina's paraphernalia was old-fashioned even for that day, and it took much ingenuity to fit her bulky box camera and tripod along the staircases and under the low arches of the Colonial building."[3]

We know little of Tina's emotional and sexual involvements after Guerrero had left for the Soviet Union. We know from details revealed later that she had indeed professed her love for Guerrero. A woman like Tina, aware of her own sexuality, might indeed have enjoyed other encounters outside of the conventionalities of her time, going her own way, and obeying the passions within her.

Often she would work with the chief editor of *El Machete,* Rosendo Gómez Lorenzo. This newspaper had become the official periodical of the Mexican Communist Party. Tina volunteered to translate from Italian to Spanish, working directly with Gómez Lorenzo. He tells of an evening in the newspaper office when Tina was translating an article, with him typing and correcting as he went. Julio Antonio Mella entered the office and a formal introduction was made. Tina had met Mella before at a demonstration on the occasion of the execution of Sacco and Vanzetti and had known of Mella's political activity in his native Cuba. Gómez Lorenzo was aware of the mutual attraction of the two and invited Mella to join them for a coffee after their work was finished. They then accompanied Tina to her home at 31 Calle Abraham González where she had been living alone. This was in June 1928; by the end of September of that year Mella was living with Tina.

Julio Antonio Mella, a young Cuban revolutionary, had been active since his student days in Havana against the dictatorial government of General Gerardo Machado (1925–1933). He had fled Cuba alone (his wife refusing to join him) and had sought refuge in Mexico. He was a student of law at the Universidad Nacional in Mexico and worked as a journalist.

In Mexico he found new emotions, and in Tina he found the woman to

courage and accompany a man of action. Their love flowered from the time
and the place, and was nurtured by the fine comradeship of belonging together
in the Communist Party. They were individuals too and each constituted for the
other a pledge for the future. After Weston, it seems as though Tina
could only love a man who was fighting to change the world.

A battle fought with the heart is the most searing, and in making the choice
of Mella over Guerrero, Tina found more than a comrade, more than a fellow
artist. Guerrero was an inscrutable, impassive man; his solid frame and
copper-hued skin belonged not to a man of action but to that strange brooding
intensity of the Mexican Indian. He was a silent man; his gestures had an
eloquence beyond words. If the basis of her personal commitments had become
primarily political, given her own inner drives and sexuality and Mella's own
obvious vitality, then the eventual transference of her affections from Guerrero
to Mella is understandable. Mella, a young hero-figure among the left in his
own country and in Mexico, had been forced into exile to pursue his dedication
to a political cause. This guiding philosophy, together with the undeniable
sexual attraction, might have provided complete fulfillment for Tina at this time
of her life. She was alone, in the full bloom of her beauty, and by this time
probably more easily accepting the changing realities of her life than she had
been previously. It was not the adventure of loving that Tina pursued, it was
love itself.

On the evening of January 10, 1929, anxious to see an issue of *El Machete*
which contained an important article by him, Mella arrived at Rosendo Gómez
Lorenzo's office and carried off the first copy. He mentioned to the editor that
he had a rendezvous at a bar with José Magriña, another Cuban, who said he
had some information about a possible attempt on Mella's life. Gómez Lorenzo
warned him to be careful, saying that it might be something else. (Magriña
later denied that this conversation had taken place.) Mella kept the
appointment and later went to meet Tina at the cable office, reporting to her
that the information he had received was vague and of no importance. Upon
leaving the cable office, shortly after 11 p.m., Mella and Tina walked toward
their apartment which was close by. Two shots were fired at Mella, the bullets
penetrating the stomach and the thorax and left shoulder. Bleeding profusely,
Mella staggered a few steps and then fell, breaking his left arm. He did not die
instantly. An ambulance brought him to the Hospital San Jerónimo; an
operation was performed in an attempt to save his life, but at 2.15 a.m. he
died. He had said in those few moments of consciousness on the pavement,
with Tina hovering over him, that it was Magriña and his political enemies who
were the assassins. The rendezvous at "La India" was a setup to enable the
assassins to follow Mella's movements.

In the following days, the right-wing press relentlessly pursued the case,

exploiting it in the most sensational fashion. It is revealing to see how one suc
paper, *Excelsior*, today more liberal, used its columns without fear of libel
or without any consciousness of journalistic ethics. The editor reiterated the
paper's unbiased reporting and immediately announced that Tina's version of
the assassination contradicted the police version. The first morning
headlines began:

FIRST REPORT OF MELLA SHOOTING
The Cuban Journalist Antonio Mella Gravely Wounded Last Night
Sr. Mella was hit by two bullets, one in the abdomen, double, penetrating the
stomach and thorax, and the other in the left shoulder. In addition he suffered
broken arm when he hit the pavement after being wounded by the well-aimed
bullets. According to information from friends of the victim immediately after th
shooting, we learned that Julio Antonio Mella spent last night working in his
office at 89 Isabel la Católica until just after eight o'clock when he suddenly
told Sra. Modotti that he was in a hurry to meet Sr. José Magriña. Sr. Mella,
accompanied by Sra. Modotti, went to see Sr. Magriña with whom he discussed
several pending matters. After leaving Sr. Magriña, Mella took care of a few
other errands, arriving near his home at about 10 o'clock...There, suddenly he
was attacked by two individuals who shot him, leaving him in agony on
the sidewalk.

The next day's headline screamed that the assassination of Mella had produce
a sensation in the capital and went on to add:
WHAT THE CUBAN STUDENT SAID BEFORE DYING
What Sra. Modotti says
Speaking at the sixth precinct, Sra. Modotti first gave another name, an
American one, and then, afterwards, her own. In her first deposition
she maintained that the two individuals had fired from a passing car. Then she
said that they had been on foot and had shot from behind, close enough for
her to smell the gunpowder; nevertheless she has given no description of the
criminals. Sra. Modotti's insistence on not naming the assassins gives rise
to suspicions that she either knows the murderer of her lover, or knows who it
was who ordered his murder. It is also said that there was one killer, and
not two, as can be seen from the bullet holes, which are one above the other;
had there been accomplices, the holes would be in different directions...

TINA HAS TRUE KEY TO CRIME was the accusatory headline in the Monda
edition of the paper:
...according to police investigations, she is the one to have supplied the motive
for the case, making it seem to have been a political crime. According to
police officials, if the motive of the murder was not "passion," Tina Modotti
must in any case know its cause and origin; if it was political, it is believed
that the Italian (T. M.) must have been an instrument of enemies of the

uban Communist.

Mella's lover is an extremely intelligent person; she is a woman who seems to be made of steel wrapped in skin: she is impenetrable, hermetic, closed to everything she doesn't want — or which is inconvenient for her — to say. If Tina Modotti insists on not telling the truth, we doubt any human effort will succeed in getting her to change her story, with her intelligence and with the ingenuousness with which she knows how to use her black eyes and flutter her lashes.

It is not hard to imagine how this kind of reporting affected Tina. The police had raided her apartment and had confiscated letters and photographs; she was virtually under house arrest, guarded by two security agents. This reference to her use of "female wiles" at a moment when she was decimated by grief, daily subjected to vile accusations in court and in the press, must have been still another blow to her dignity and added to her contempt for the reporters. In the same edition of *Excelsior*, there appeared a telegram sent by Portes Gil, then President of Mexico, who had been outside of Mexico City on the night of the murder, to the Secretary of the Communist Party of Mexico, assuring him of a complete investigation of the assassination. The next day, the 5th, *Excelsior* printed a scurrilous editorial:

ASPECTS OF A SENSATIONAL CRIME

The murder of the Communist student, Julio Antonio Mella, has caused great excitement in this city, in the whole country, and in Cuba. Until the present time, however, the criminal remains unknown because the only person who could identify him or give circumstantial evidence — the dead man's lover — remains suspiciously silent, declaring that she "did not see" the assailant, although the victim was shot at close range.

The crime would have been an ordinary one and would have attracted the public's attention only briefly, were it not for the fact that the Cuban government has been accused of the serious charge of homicide and complicity in the crime because Mella was an enemy of General Machado. Even the Cuban ambassador, Mr. Mascaro, has been hurt by the accusations, although those who made them are a group of people without any representation amongst us, and who are notorious for the passion and virulence of their openly demagogic and anti-social tendencies.

Our government has shown impartiality and judiciousness; it has pledged protection to the Cuban embassy in the event of possible attacks by Communists — who pretend to glorify Julio Antonio Mella as the martyr of a redeeming idea. It has also ordered the police to actively carry out its investigations of the case so that it may be solved and the criminal may not remain unpunished.

We do not prejudge, nor do we hypothesize; it is up to the police and the courts to clarify the circumstances of the crime. Meanwhile, we shall observe the prudent and impartial attitude that behooves an honorable newspaper. We shall, nevertheless, continue to inform our readers, as we have in the past, of the progress of the case and of its final outcome. The Cuban government maintains the most sincere and cordial diplomatic relations with our government. Both Cubans and Mexicans have common origins; both deserve our deepest respect. It would not be right that just because of the prejudiced and one-sided declarations of those opposed to General Machado and because Mella was his enemy, we should side with those who, without any proof, disturb the authorities of that country by accusing them of such a heinous crime.

In contrast to that attitude, those who in Mexico boast of being Communists; those who have their eyes fixed on Russia, as if it were the cradle and source of new civilization; those who without patriotism or national solidarity are ready to submit themselves to the government of an alien regime and to accept the protection of any demagogue as long as he consorts with the Jewery of Russian Bolshevism; those Mexicans who ally themselves with nomadic foreigners, took advantage of the situation to declare emphatically, but gratuitously, that Mella was a victim of the Cuban government, a victim sacrificed on the altar of an ideal, deserving, thus, of consecration in the eyes of the world and of history.

In accordance with such a declaration, Communist groups (of both sexes, because women also participated) have assumed a hostile and injurious attitude against the Cuban government and its ambassador in Mexico. They add insult to injury by bringing up the well-worn theme of Yankee imperialism, and affirm that Mexico's press has sold out to the gold of Wall Street. As the Communists accuse General Machado and his representative amongst us of the latter charge, it must be emphasized that the indictment is ridiculous and absurd.

We have seen two extremely revealing photographs picked up by the police. One of Julio Antonio Mella and the other of his lover, Tina Modotti. Both photographs show these individuals completely naked, in an indecent pose that would be acceptable in shameless criminals and underworld figures, but not in an "apostle" of Communism, a redeemer of the people, or in his protecting nymph, Egeria — the guide and inspiration of the noble revolutionary.

And this fact — just this one — would suffice for upright and decent people to deprive Mella of posthumous honors and to relegate his mistress to the category of females who sell their love.

Is it not a folly to take Mella's side against the Cuban government when there is no basis to accuse the latter of the former's death? Where do the Communists demonstrations and public injury come from? Have our police authorities perhaps given proof of partiality?

Let us await the judgment of the law and let us not anticipate reprehensible outbursts. Maybe this was a crime of passion and not a political one. If that were the case, isn't all this high-sounding oratory ridiculous; aren't the diatribes against the Cuban authorities unjust; and aren't the demonstrations of our "reds" and "red-blacks" unjust?

Interior of church tower, Tepotzotlan, by Tina Modotti, 1924
Collection: Archivo Fotográfico Histórico, Pachuca

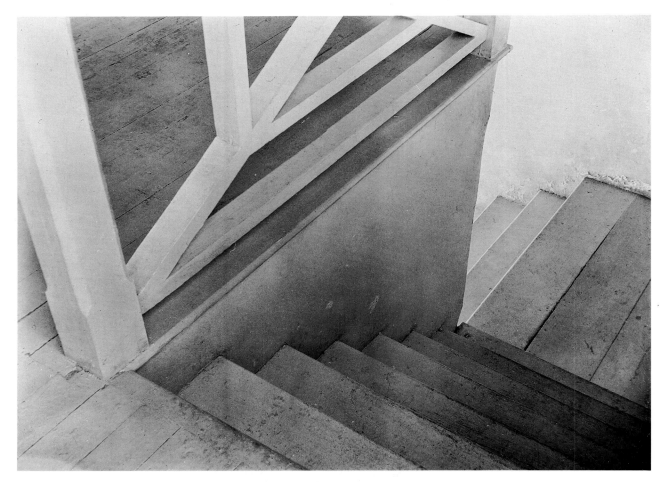

Staircase, by Tina Modotti
Collection: The Museum of Modern Art, New York

Stadium, by Tina Modotti
Collection: The Museum of Modern Art, New York

Telephone lines, by Tina Modotti, c. 1928–29
Collection: Comitato Tina Modotti, Trieste

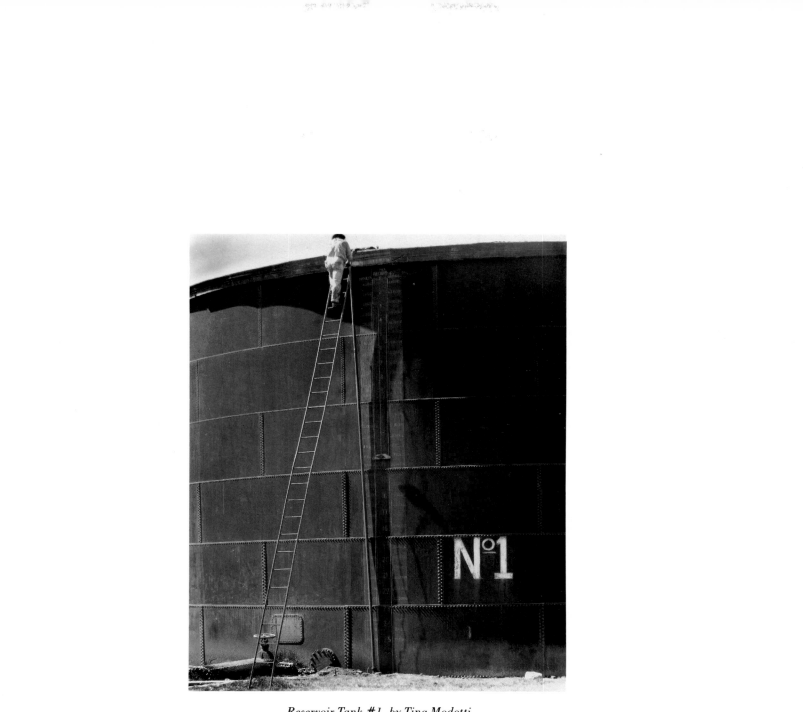

Reservoir Tank #1, by Tina Modotti
Collection: Comitato Tina Modotti, Trieste

Convent of Tepotzotlan, Mexico, by Tina Modotti
Collection: The Museum of Modern Art,
New York

Doorway Arch, by Tina Modotti
Collection: Comitato Tina Modotti, Trieste

Women of Tehuantepec, by Tina Modotti
Collection: Archivo Fotográfico Histórico, Pachuca

Easter lily and bud, by Tina Modotti
Collection: The Museum of Modern Art, New York

Calla Lily, by Tina Modotti, 1927
Collection: The Museum of Modern Art, New York

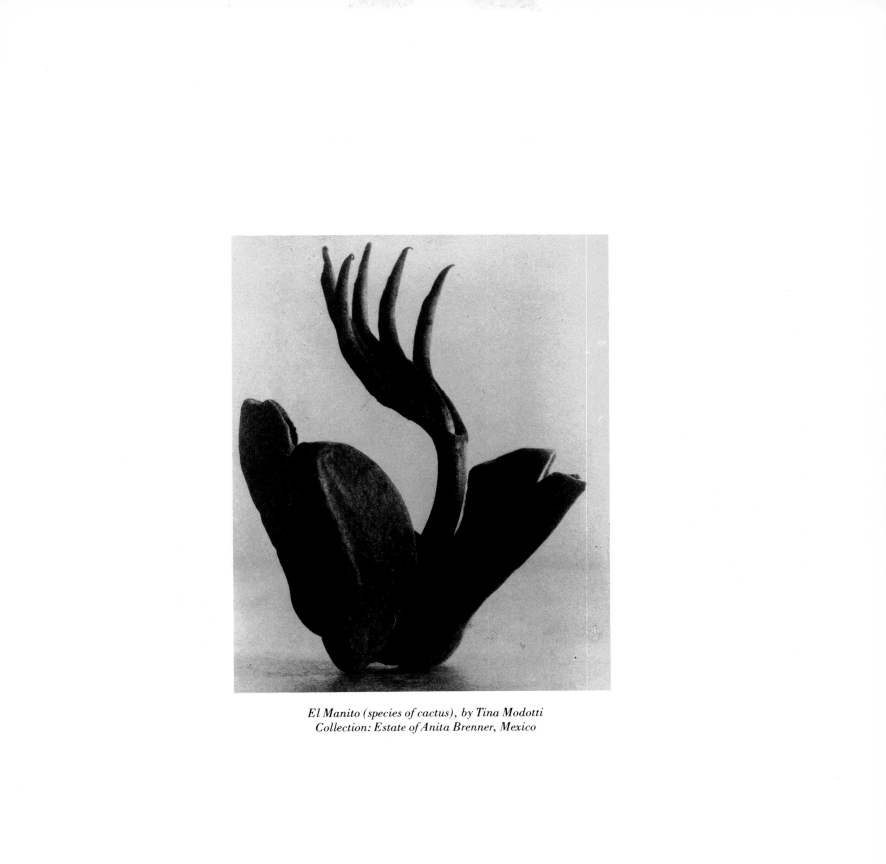

El Manito (species of cactus), by Tina Modotti
Collection: Estate of Anita Brenner, Mexico

Roses, Mexico, by Tina Modotti, 1924
Collection: The Museum of Modern Art, New York

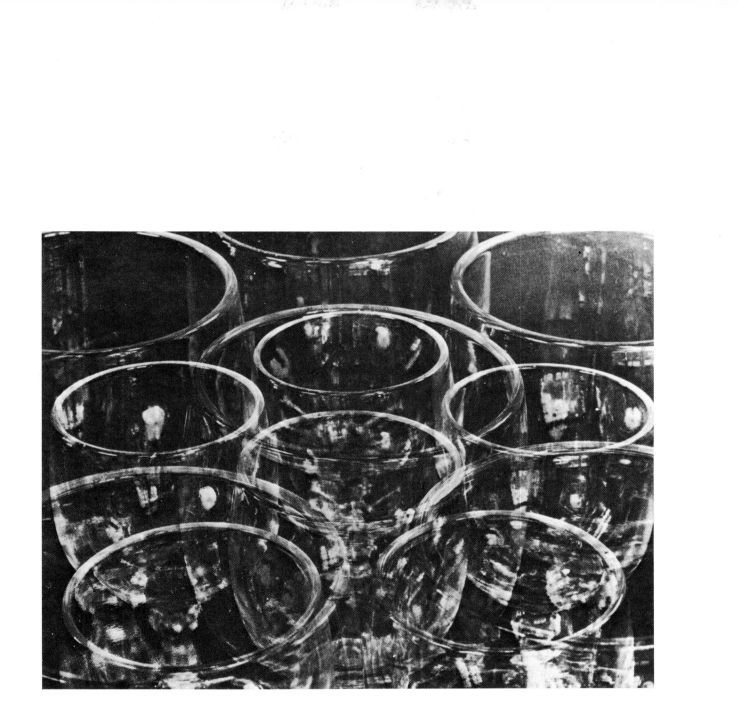

Wine Glasses, by Tina Modotti, 1925
Collection: Mills College Art Gallery, Oakland, California

And the gold of Wall Street? Where is that famous gold, coveted by shabby individuals who feign to disdain it because they don't have any? The gold of Wall Street that corrupts the Mexican press! It must be like the sincerity of our Communists and the untarnished virtue of Tina Modotti.

In the same edition, *Excelsior* in its efforts to be "impartial," interviewed thirty people, none of whom believed it was a crime of passion. "'The serious part is that while they're trying to build up a case for the idea of a crime of passion they're losing time in the investigation. And it is quite possible that with this method,' the painter Diego Rivera told us, 'the remaining traces will be lost and the murderer will escape.'" At another point in the interview, Rivera said, "I also warned Mella to watch out, since he had received word that he was being followed by assassins. I even asked him to do me the favor of staying in at night. I thought it would be good to take precautions, and that he should always be accompanied by two young men from the Party, just in case. But since he was careless and brave, he paid no attention."

In discussing the Colt 45 pistol which was believed to be the murder weapon, and which had been said to have been in the possession of Tina Modotti, the American journalist Carleton Beals gave the newspaper a detailed account. *About four months ago, Mr. Lee Simonson Jr., editor of the New York art magazine* Creative Art, *wrote to me asking for material on the Mexican art scene, because he wanted to devote a special issue to the art of this country. Among other things, he wanted me to write an article on the photography of Tina Modotti and to send him all her best photographs so that he could reproduce them. I sent him the article, which as a matter of fact will be appearing in the next issue of the magazine. As soon as I received Mr. Simonson's letter I went to Tina's house to gather information and photographs. While I was getting the former, Fritz Bach, a German journalist, came by, and in the course of talking about various subjects not worth mentioning, Tina picked up a pistol that was on the work table and placed it in Bach's hands. He examined it, and I could tell he was interested in buying it. Mr. Bach tried to take it apart, but he couldn't. He asked Tina how the weapon worked and she told him she didn't know. Then Bach turned to me and asked me to show him, but since I don't know anything about guns I couldn't help him out.*

Excelsior also interviewed Gloria and Max Campbell, who lived in the same house as Modotti. They heard Mella's cries, as did another woman, who operates a bakery close by on the same street. She thought the shots she had heard were tire blow-outs. On opening her window, she saw a boy running, and she heard Mella say that Machado and the Cuban Embassy were responsible for his death. She ran to the phone and called the Green Cross. *Excelsior* continued:

In the final analysis," according to one source, "Mella would have said nothing once he was mortally wounded, because he wouldn't have wanted to compromise Tina." According to sources who know Sra. Modotti through having cultivated her friendship, said lady is not of an age capable of exciting violent passions. She has been accustomed from an early age to earning her own living and to living independently — due to the fact that she was raised and educated in the United States; and, rather than unchecked love, she has brought respect and intellectual devotion to those she calls her "companions." Among the latter, we heard the names — Mella was the last — of men who were by no means uncultivated but, on the contrary, had a total awareness of life. For them, Modotti has not been the physical woman, but the special, preferred friend who understood and stimulated them. Her socialist ideas — we were told — are sufficient explanation for her alliance with Mella. "Tina," said one of the group we interviewed, "never allowed herself to be dominated by a man in the ordinary sense of the word; yes, for a man with a mind she would have affection, a meeting of spirits; but nothing more."

Sr. Gómez Lorenzo had denied in an interview that Mella ever received money from Magriña. He asserted that Mella answered Magriña's call because he wanted to find out how things were going in Cuba.

Sr. Lorenzo had warned Mella to be very careful with Magriña, because Magriña came from a suspicious political background and it wouldn't be at all surprising if he were a spy for the Cuban government.

The article continued:

Regarding the conduct — way of life — of Julio Antonio Mella, his friends told us yesterday that he was so involved in political propaganda work, projects he was either creating or directing — constantly giving conferences, attending meetings, editing correspondence — that they don't understand how he found time for all his activities.

To summarize: the friends and co-workers of Mella maintain that it is not a case of a crime of passion and that even though the investigation being conducted by Mexican authorities is pursuing this course, they should not abandon the idea that it was a political crime.

On January 16, accompanied by Diego Rivera as well as by the security agent who was vigilant in his "guarding" of her, Tina arrived in court for an official interrogation which was carried verbatim by the paper:

Q. On what date did you first meet Julio Antonio Mella?
A. I can't tell you exactly, but it was during the Sacco and Vanzetti campaign, at the beginning of last year, in this city. Not that at the time we were close; I had been introduced to him and we would say hello to each other, that's all.

121

Q. On what date did he first ask you to make love with him?

A. Last year, in June; I agreed last September.

Q. Were you involved with anyone else at the time?

A. I was not spiritually tied to any other person when I liked and loved Mella. Before that I had ended a previous commitment.

Q. Do you know Xavier Guerrero?

A. Yes, I met him in Los Angeles, California, where he had been asked by the Secretary of Industry to mount an exhibition of popular art in 1923.

Q. What were his political ideas?

A. He was and is a Communist, affiliated with the Mexican Communist party.

Q. Who do you think had stronger ideas about Communism, Mella or Guerrero

A. Both.

Q. Are you sure?

A. Absolutely.

Q. Don't you consider it a violation of a person or of a love to write love letters to someone else? In other words, being in an intimate relationship with one person, don't you abuse him in writing of love to someone else?

A. Yes.

Q. Did you love Guerrero very much?

A. In his time, yes.

Q. Can you tell us whether Guerrero was very much in love with you?

A. Yes, I can. But the love he had for me was less than the love he had for the fundamental love of his life, the revolution. He was ready to die for it.

Q. Do you believe that when someone feels love for someone, he is willing to sacrifice her for another?

A. If the person is worthy, yes. The love of revolutionaries is not separate from their other activities; it is related to their political ideals.

Q. When you began to have intimate relations with Mella, did you break off completely with Guerrero?

A. Yes. That is to say, I kept sending him weekly newspapers for his activities.

Q. And you didn't send him any letters?

A. Absolutely not. Only periodicals. I wanted him to be up to date on politics in general in Mexico.

Q. What was the form of the break-up between yourself and Guerrero?

A. A definitive letter.

Q. Did you ever tell Mella about your relationship with Guerrero?

A. Yes, right at the beginning, because I was going through a tremendous conflict. Mella didn't understand the struggles I had to go through to reach a point where I could decide to be his companion. Those months of hesitation were incomprehensible to him, and he interpreted them differently. It's not exactly that I was hesitating because I still loved Guerrero...In fact, after Xavier had been gone a week, I thought about it at length and I freely resolved to stay with Mella.

The judge, Attorney Pino Cámara, wound up the examination of the witness with the following question:

Q. *When Guerrero left, did you have any other suitors?*
A. *No, none.*

The deposition finished, Tina Modotti was escorted back to her house by the agent. *Excelsior* continued its coverage with the following:
Wasn't it a crime of passion? It is possible, since, of those under suspicion by the police, one is the dead man himself, who with his double personality (Julio Antonio Mella used this name in Mexico — his name in Cuba was N. McPartland) facilitated the betrayal; and the other, Señor X, is still in Moscow and is the painter Xavier Guerrero, the first lover of Tina Modotti. Whether it be political or whether it had a different motive, the Mella murder will only be understood if the Venetian Tina Modotti decides to break the impenetrable silence, the firm hermeticism within which she has locked herself, and reveals the identity of the mysterious person who accompanied them down Avenida Morelos, along the Paseo de la Reforma, and into Abraham Gonzalez, where he fired the two shots that killed her friend.

The newspaper had in some way obtained copies of two letters: one in which Mella spoke of his intense love for Tina, the other a carbon of a letter from Tina, the original of which was sent to Señor X, Xavier Guerrero (to whom that pseudonym belongs),* telling him she no longer loved him because she loved another.

The newspaper quoted these letters because they considered them the basis of the investigation of Tina. The letter signed by N. McPartland (Mella) and sent by him from Oaxaca said in part:
Sept. 11, 9 p. m.
My dear Tinisima, Just a few lines after the telegram...You may feel it was careless of me to send the telegram, since you're accustomed to being terrified by what there is between us, as if it were the worst crime in the world. Nevertheless...nothing more right and more natural...and...more necessary for our life. Besides, I thought it important for you to receive these lines the very same night. No?
I haven't forgotten your face once on this whole long journey. I still see you "in mourning" — clothing and spirit — saying your last goodbye as if you wanted to come toward me...

And then appeared the text of the letter to Xavier Guerrero (written shortly after her decision to be with Mella) which also was read into the testimony:
Mexico, September 15, 1928
There is no doubt that this will be the most difficult, most painful, and most

*This salutation was of course not a pseudonym but merely the abbreviation of Xavier.

Woman, Mexico, by Tina Modotti
Collection: George Eastman House, Rochester, New York

Opposite page:
Elisa, Mexico, by Tina Modotti, 1924
Collection: The Museum of Modern Art, New York

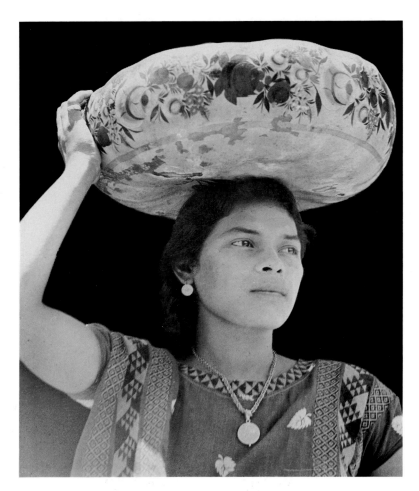

Woman of Tehuantepec, by Tina Modotti
Collection: Comitato Tina Modotti, Trieste

Next page:
Woman carrying anarcho-sindicalist black banner,
by Tina Modotti, 1928
Collection: Comitato Tina Modotti, Trieste

Above and next page:
Luz Jiménez and baby, Mexico, by Tina Modotti, 1926

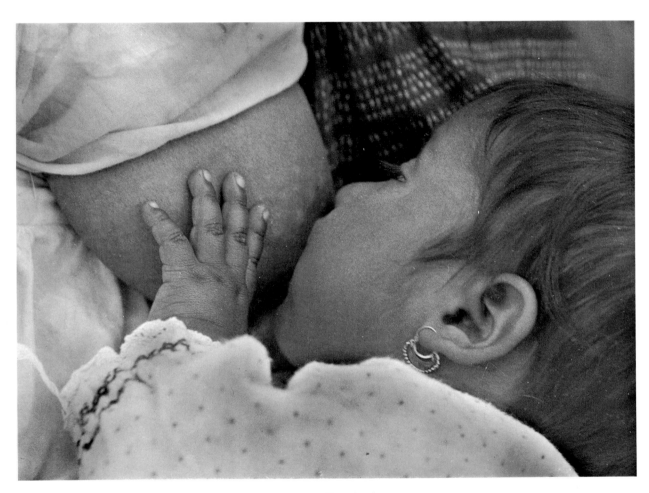

Baby nursing, by Tina Modotti, 1926

Opposite page:
Pregnant mother and child, Oaxaco,
by Tina Modotti, c. 1929
Collection: Archivo Fotográfico Histórico, Pachuca

Baby, Mexico, by Tina Modotti, c. 1926
Collection: Mr. and Mrs. Ralph Bettelheim, New York

Next page:
Muchacho with sombrero, Mexico, by Tina Modotti, c. 1927
Collection: Archivo Fotográfico Histórico, Pachuca

Mexican girl, by Tina Modotti, 1928
Collection: Archivo Fotográfico Histórico, Pachuca

Girl carrying a pail, by Tina Modotti, c. 1926
Collection: Comitato Tina Modotti, Trieste

Two children, Mexico, by Tina Modotti, 1927
Collection: Archivo Fotográfico Histórico, Pachuca

terrible letter I have ever written in my whole life. I've waited a long time before
writing it, mainly because I wanted to be very sure of the things I am going
to tell you and secondly, because I know from the start the terrible effect that th
will have on you.

I need all the calm and serenity of spirit I have to explain to you clearly, witho
ambiguities; and above all, to keep myself from getting emotional, which
would be inevitable if I let myself think of what this letter represents for you.
X., sometimes when I think of the pain I am about to cause you, I feel more lik
a monster than a human being; and I'm sure you will think this is true. At othe
times I see myself as the poor victim of a terrible fate, with a hidden force
that acts on me, despite myself, the way it acts on life. But I would be the first
reject these elements: "fate," or "hidden force," etc. Well then, what remains?
What is it that I am? Why do I act in this way? I sincerely believe that I have
intrinsically good feelings, and that I've always tried to do good for others
before I've thought of myself, not to be cruel for its own sake. That's the proof
that when I have to be the way I'm being with you now, I suffer (perhaps more
than you) because of the consequences.

But I should tell you what it is I have to tell you: I love another man. I love hir
and he loves me, and this love has made it possible for something to happen
which I thought could never happen: to stop loving you.

X., I could tell you at length the whole history of this love, how it began, how
evolved, how it reached the point where I resolved to tell you about it; how I ha
even fought with myself to extirpate it from my life (I swear to you, even to
the point of considering suicide if it could have provided a solution that would
not have been cowardly). I could tell you, in short, all the tortures caused by
this terrible dilemma I have had to face. I've thought of everything, and
principally of you (this won't offend you, I'm sure). I've thought even more of th
effect this step will have on revolutionary action. This has been my greatest
worry, greater even than my worry about you. Well, I've come to the conclusion
that however it turns out, whether I'm with you or with someone else, here or ir
some other place, whatever small use I can be to the cause — to our cause — it
will not suffer, because the work for the cause is not the reflection or the result c
loving a revolutionary, but a deep-seated conviction within me. For which I owe
you a lot, X. You were the one who opened my eyes, you were the one who help
me when I could feel the pillar of my old beliefs shaking beneath my feet. And
think that for all the help you gave me, this is how I pay you. How terrible!
X., the only thing that gives me any comfort is knowing that you are very stror
and that you will be able to overcome the pain I cause you. I ask myself now
whether you will doubt the sincerity of how I loved you. X., I swear to you on
the sacred life of my mother that I loved you as I have never loved before in
my life, and I swear to you that my feeling for you was the greatest pride of m
life. And yet despite this, what has happened has happened. How was it
possible? I myself do not know, I do not understand it, but I do feel that what

appening now is a clear and inevitable reality, and that I can do no less
than what I am doing. I thought of waiting to tell you this verbally on your
return, here; or else to go to where you are to tell you. I thought that that
would be more honest and more loyal than to tell it to you through this letter.
But I realized that to go on writing to you in the tone that was always so
natural, but which would be pretending, would mean to deceive you, and I
respect you too much for that. And also I cannot, should not, deceive
you nor betray the present reality...

What is the nature of the woman who has written this letter — a poignant,
self-searing portrayal of her true self? No heroics here, but a courage born of
honesty and bearing the burden of a love gone; the self-reproach accepted,
with an acknowledgment of a specific guilt rather than any singular acceptance
of guilt; a woman who had known love and friendship; who knew the
elusiveness of love and treasured the depths of friendship.

Letters of protest to the editorial were sent to *Excelsior* by trade unions,
women's groups and individuals, among whom were Miguel Covarrubias and
Diego Rivera. They demanded an interview with the Director of the paper,
and the following day the headline stated:

*THE PHOTOGRAPHS OF TINA MODOTTI AND JULIO A. MELLA,
ACCORDING TO VARIOUS ARTISTS*

*They are Not Immoral Pornographic Nudes But Artistic Nudes, According to
Authors of Declaration*

*(As the sign of our sincere impartiality we have made room for the following
declaration, leaving full responsibility for its ethical content up to its authors.)*
We refer to your editorial of yesterday, January 15:
*Certain photographs of nudes which were found in Tina Modotti's house led
your reporter to describe both Sra. Modotti and Julio Antonio Mella with
epithets which are an insult to the dead man and to a woman who has no way
of defending herself.*
*In addition — and this is the point which prompted our action — this attack sets
a dangerous precedent against free professional expression for artists in all
forms: in sculpture, in painting, in dance, in theater. It is impossible to maintain
that the nude in and of itself is immoral; if that were true, fifty percent of the
world's greatest works of art would have to be condemned.*
*To defend our rights as artists, we approached the most distinguished
professionals in Mexico and showed them the Modotti photographs which might
have been those referred to in your editorial. We obtained, in writing, the
opinion of all these respected artists whose reputation is well established both
artistically and morally; all of them were in favor of artistic nudes and
against the opinion expressed in your editorial.*
These written opinions were brought last night to the offices of Excelsior, *after
we had asked that they be published in the name of impartiality; but we were*

*Shortly after Tina's arrival in the Soviet Union
she went to see Xavier Guerrero who was living
at the Hotel Lux. Vittorio Vidali reports that
when she returned from this visit he found her in
a withdrawn saddened state. It appears that
Tina wanted to talk to Guerrero about all that
had transpired since her last letter to him written
in 1928. Guerrero, mute and solemn as always,
listened without comment. However on Tina's
leave-taking he indicated that he would prefer to
think that their acquaintance was over and that
what had happened in the past did not exist.*

told that this was impossible since the edition was already closed. Today, the 16th, at noon, we returned to Excelsior *with the written opinions and the proof of all the nude photographs taken by Tina Modotti, which we did not believe to be the ones upon which your columnist had based his conclusions. We asked see the ones he had used, but Señor Espinosa said he did not think he could comply with our request. He arranged an appointment for us at 6 o'clock with Señor Rodrigo de Llano, director of* Excelsior, *to discuss the matter. We were warmly received by Sr. de Llano, who was kind enough to show us the photographs in question. One of them shows Julio Antonio Mella naked in fron of a shower door, and was taken to fulfill the entrance requirements of a rowin club in Havana. Julio Antonio Mella, who was one of the best rowers in that city, must have had the picture taken just as athletes all over the world have th pictures taken in sports clubs all over the world. This photograph was taken ov three years ago, before he had even heard of Tina Modotti, who obviously had nothing to do with it. As far as the other photograph is concerned, it is an artistic nude, the work of a photographer Edward Weston, who is recognized a the greatest artist in his field in America today. Sra. Modotti posed for the photograph, working as a professional model for her teacher, Weston.*

We asked Sr. de Llano why the documents of an investigation — which is the only way these photographs could have been requisitioned by the police — happened to be in the editorial offices of Excelsior *and not in court or in the offices of the police, Sr. de Llano replied that* Excelsior *had received these photographs anonymously. The fact that, as Sr. de Llano told us, the photographs were conveyed anonymously to* Excelsior, *shows exactly the intentions of whoever sent them; the fact that they were not taken by either Tin Modotti or Julio Antonio Mella converts the assertions and interpretations contained in yesterday's editorial into* absolute *lies with no value whatsoever. The director of* Excelsior, *with whom we discussed all these points in our meeting with him, has kindly offered to publish this declaration. We hope it wil be inserted in a position equivalent to that occupied by the editorial to which w have repeatedly referred. In advance, our deep thanks to Sr. Rodrigo de Llano.*

Mexico, D. F., January 16, 1929
Miguel Covarrubias
Diego Rivera

Excelsior *printed their interview with Magriña:*
"But we have also been told that when Mella fell down wounded he said that you knew everything..."
"Nobody has heard that he says that."
"Tina Modotti assures it."
"Don't you think they've been irresponsible not to have followed out the possibility that Tina Modotti is a Fascist spy, and that Xavier Guerrero, the ma

of the letters, is in Moscow? Couldn't there have been a plan on the part of Mella's own friends? They say Modotti has been a Fascist spy..."

And turning to certain details of the slaying, to the exact moment when it was carried out, *Excelsior's* reporter asked Magriña to give his opinion on the veracity of Tina's statement that it was impossible for her to see the assailant. Magriña declared Tina to be lying, adding that in his opinion, "When a person is attacked from behind, the first thing he or she does is to turn around to see who it is. At least that's what I would do, even if I was arm in arm with my father and I had to attend to him after seeing that he had just been wounded."

The reporter explained to Magriña that one of the most serious charges against him was that it appeared very plausible that he could have followed Mella home after their meeting, or that he was already waiting for them at the site where Mella was shot.
"Have you seen," we asked him, "Diego Rivera's accusations against you which appeared in one of the morning papers?"
"This man Rivera doesn't even know what I look like, to go around making accusations like that. All the accusations that have been made against me are of that type. I can't give them any importance. When I come before a judge, then they'll see all their lies destroyed, one by one."

Pepe Magriña had been apprehended and imprisoned briefly as the agent-provocateur behind the assassination. The police had found the newspaper *El Machete* on Mella's body, as well as a paper bearing Magriña's address and telephone number, but he denied that he had sought the rendezvous and that it was indeed Mella who approached him regarding the newspaper *Cuba Libre*. He was later released.

For Tina, the damage had been done. Her name had finally been cleared. The complicity of the Machado government, together with the apparent complicity of the Mexican police, was recognized, and it brought about the dismissal of the Chief of Police in charge of the investigation. Relations with Cuba were ruptured by the withdrawal of the Cuban ambassador. But the blatant accusations of the editorial, compounded by the indignities of the cross-examinations hurled at her at the hearings, started a vendetta of slander in the rightist press that continued and indeed was to reappear at the time of Tina's death twelve years later. She must have written the details of this period to Weston: his entry for the day February 21 in his Daybook states that he has received "a letter from Tina disclosing her strength through a terrible ordeal: she has maintained and proved her innocence."

After only four months of a fulfilling and rewarding relationship, Tina was left alone again to face not only the loss of a love but the vilification of her whole life. Yet when she wrote in March to Weston, her first thoughts were about Brett, who had broken his leg in an accident. "Monna just told me of the terrible news about Brett. I am so upset that I cannot think clearly — is he better? Will his leg be normal again? Poor boy, I cannot quite grasp this misfortune — it seems so terrible! Please give him my deepest sympathy and tell him I feel for him with all my heart! And for you, Edward, too! I know how much you must feel and suffer! I have gone through so much suffering myself lately and my heart is so full of pain and bleeding that it makes me all the more receptive to the suffering of the beings which are dear to me."

The letter continued:

Oh Edward, for a few moments to be near you — to be able to give vent to all the pent-up emotions which gnaw at my heart — you might not agree with all I would say — that does not matter — but you would understand the tragedy of my soul and feel with me — and that, not everybody can do!

But I cannot afford the luxury of even my sorrows today — I well know this is no time for tears; the most is expected from us and we must not slacken — not stop halfway — the rest is impossible — neither our consciences nor the memory of the dead victims would allow us that — I am living in a different world, Edward — strange how this very city and country can seem so utterly different to me than seemed years ago! At times I wonder if I have really changed so much myself or if it is just a kind of superstructure laid over me. Of course I have changed my convictions, of that there is no doubt in the least, but in regards to mode of living, tastes, new habits, etc. — are they just a result of living in a certain environment, or have they really taken the place of the old life? I did not make this very clear; I mean: are these new habits taken up in order to keep pace with the new environment, or have they really taken the place of the old life? I have never stopped to question this before and I cannot understand why I am doing it now; I guess dear it was just a desire to talk with you a while like in the old times... P.S. There is something I have been forgetting to tell you in my last letters — Things are very insecure here for "pernicious foreigners." I am prepared for the worst — any day they may apply the "33" on us — I want to have all my things in shape as much as possible. What shall I do with all your negatives?*

What is underneath this questioning of herself? There does not appear to be regret for either the demands or the consequences of the political life she has chosen. Perhaps this is a moment when she is overcome by the events of the last year and, as was her custom, her letters to Weston become a sounding board for the questioning and clarification of her own thinking.

Tina was continuing to make her livelihood through photography. Her photographic eye was much in demand. She had the priceless ability to intuit nd communicate. At the same time she was able to record the essence of time and place with clarity and discernment. In a sense hers was an original ye, seeing Mexico not from the viewpoint of an outsider, but with a ompassion and personal knowledge and involvement. Her work had been used n the magazine *Mexican Folkways* since 1927, even outside of Mexico her ork was much sought after. She received invitations from the *British Journal f Photography* and Pacific International Salon of Photographic Art. he *Revue Mensuelle Illustré* "Varietés" in Brussels published her work as did e art magazine *Creative Art*, in New York, with an article by Carleton eals which appeared in February 1929. Requests for her photographs came om Prague as well, and the Agfa Paper Company sought her endorsement f their photographic paper (August 1929).

September of 1929 she reported to Weston:

am still in Mexico but it is so disagreeable not to know how much longer one is lowed to remain, it makes it almost impossible to make plans for work, but of urse the wisest attitude is to simply go on, do everything one intends to do as if thing was ever going to happen to spoil one's plans...I am thinking strongly give an exhibit here in the near future; I feel that if I leave the country, I most owe it to the country to show, not so much what I have done here, but pecially what can be done without resorting to colonial churches and charros d chinas poblanas, and similar trash most photographers have indulged in. on't you think so, dear? By the way, had I ever told you that I was offered the sition of official photographer of the National Museum some months back? ell, tempting as the offer was, I could not accept it. Many have criticized me r the refusal, but both as a member of the party and as companion to Mella, it uld have been impossible. The government here did absolutely nothing to ing about justice when they had all the opportunity in the world; they had the ost responsible guilty one in their hands and they let him go free. Anyway, far as work is concerned, I have always plenty of it, in fact more than I can , considering that I cannot give all my time to photography.

bviously, Tina's strength and personal convictions allowed for no compromise. n November 5th in a letter signed by the artists Carlos Orozco and Carlos érida on behalf of the *Dirección de Acción Cívica* of the Federal District of exico, Tina was formally invited to present her work, and she accepted the pportunity. The exhibition was inaugurated by the Rector of the *Universidad acional Autónoma de México* in the National Library, and Tina's work was uded in many publications; several photographs were reproduced and she as hailed as an original force in photography. One of the most important mments came from Gustavo Ortíz Hernán, then a young critic, now Director *El Universal Gráfico*. He stated:

ithout a doubt the photographs of Tina Modotti are highly personal and

145

Men reading El Machete, *signed by Tina Modotti, 1924*
Collection: Archivo Fotográfico Histórico, Pachuca

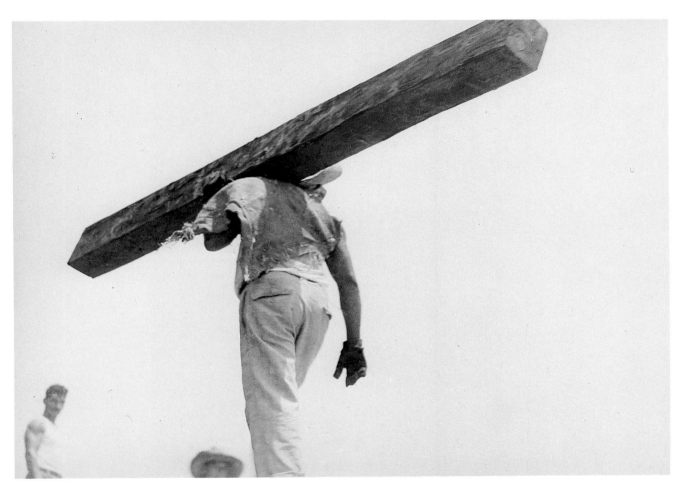

Mexican worker, by Tina Modotti, 1928
Collection: The Museum of Modern Art, New York

Loading bananas on a ship, Vera Cruz, by Tina Modotti, 1928
Collection: Archivo Fotográfico Histórico, Pachuca

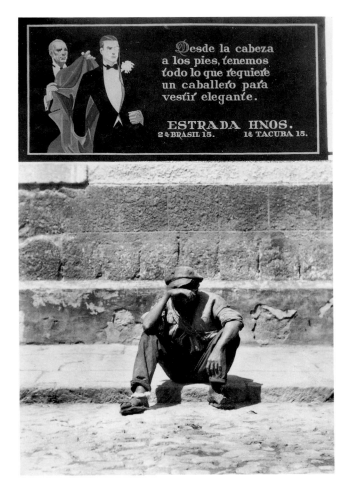

Elegance and Poverty, by Tina Modotti
Collection: Comitato Tina Modotti, Trieste

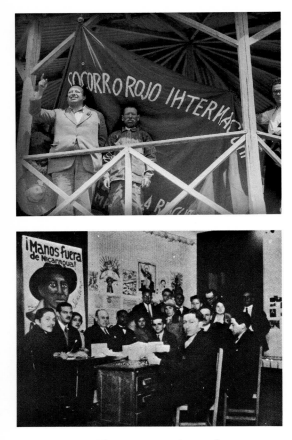

Diego Rivera addressing a meeting at the International Red Aid, Mexico, by Tina Modotti, c.1928

Meeting of the Hands-off Nicaragua Committee, Mexico, by Tina Modotti, 1926

distinct. Ideologically she belongs to the avant garde and the extreme tendencie of the social movement of which she is counted among the most significant followers. Her integrity and her courage were demonstrated on the occasion of the assassination of Julio Antonio Mella. Her photographs can be easily classified: works of pure composition in which concerns for perspective, construction and dimension reveal the skill of the artist in handling her mediur. Composition of flowers, of jars, of tools form a special kind of still life handled with great plasticity. There are two special photographs which should be given the title of "Revolution"— a perfect synthesis of a great social ideology: an ear c corn, the neck of a guitar, and a cartridge belt (see p. 92) are juxtaposed in one; in the other, a sickle takes the place of the guitar — the photographic qualities undiminished by the substitution.

In another category is a particularly magnificent photograph — a group of crystal wine glasses is composed (see p. 119), their photogenic qualities combined with a rhythm and musicality which is attained by an association of ideas. The power of suggestion is enormous in this photograph — the perfect synchronization of transparencies is magnificent. In another group, the scenes c our daily lives — construction sites, stairs, stadium, wires — which we look at indifferently — acquire an almost exotic prestige and a unique personality. The photographs of Tina Modotti are symbolic of the eagerness and anxiety of the new young to know everything, to examine everything and to revise it.

On the occasion of the exhibition and publication of her own work, Tina had said, "I consider myself a photographer, nothing more... Photography, precisely because it can only be produced in the present and because it is based on what exists objectively before the camera, takes its place as the most satisfactory medium of registering life in all its aspects, and from this comes its documental value. If to this is added sensibility and understanding and, above all, a clear orientation as to the place it should have in the field of historical development, I believe that the result is something worthy of a place in social production, to which we should all contribute." This viewpoint is particularly important when we learn later of her reactions to street life in Berlin and her stated inability to function as a reporter. She was dedicated to an expression in which aesthetic and political sensibilities were united.

Tina's exhibition attracted accolades not only from her fellow artists, but also from the thousands of workers who passed in awe before her irrefutable denunciations of the living conditions of the poor. David Alfaro Siqueiros, before the end of the exhibition, gave a lecture on December 14, 1929, under the title, "The First Revolutionary Photographic Exhibition in Mexico." Describing the strength and beauty of Tina's work, he spoke of the true meaning of photography in Mexico — "the art form which mirrored and retaine what it saw and offered through the purity of her expression the surprise of

eing able to look at what the viewer had previously only seen." Tina reported
o Weston, "I wish you had heard S's conference. It was great. Such profound
nowledge of the history of art through the ages and such a vital and
ignificant viewpoint. We were surely smart in getting the program presented.
But after the government, the University and all the Mexican politicos pride
hemselves on their *revolucionarismo*, they couldn't very well refuse."

Of great interest to the artists and intellectuals, not only in Mexico but
hroughout Europe and the United States, came the news of Diego Rivera's
xpulsion from the Communist Party in the autumn of 1929. There had
ever been a logical, official, or even a personally coherent account from Diego
imself as to the causes of the break. Even as late as 1961, Bertram Wolfe
ndicates in his *The Fabulous Life of Diego Rivera* that "the causes were
nternational in origin. Diego was caught in a world-wide purge emanating from
actional politics in the Soviet Union, involving in some countries the
xclusion of whole parties, in others expulsion or resignation of the principal
eaders and founders..." He goes on to add that Diego was also accused
y his fellow party members of "working on the public buildings of a bourgeois
overnment, and of accepting from its hands the post of director of the School
f Plastic Art." This expulsion was the kind of news which Tina would most
aturally report to Weston, as well as reporting Diego's marriage to "a lovely
ineteen-year-old girl of German father and Mexican mother, a painter herself,"
'rida Kahlo:

*Tina accompanied by Diego Rivera on way to police
hearings, Mexico, 1929*

*ut the most startling news about D. is another one which will be spread through
ll the corners of the world tomorrow. No doubt you will know of it before this
etter reaches you. Diego is out of the party. Only last night the decision was
aken. Reasons? That his many jobs he has lately accepted from the government,
ecorating the National Palace of Fine Arts, are incompatible with a militant
ember of the party. Still the party did not ask him to leave his posts, all they
sked him was to make a public statement that the holding of these jobs did not
revent him from fighting the present reactionary government. His whole
ttitude lately has been a very passive one in regard to the party, and he would
ot sign the statement so out he went. There was no alternative.
here are so many sides to this question. We all know that he is a much greater
ainter than he is a militant member of the party, so the party did not ask him
 give up painting, all they asked him was to make that statement and live up
 it. We all know that all these positions were thrust upon him by the
overnment precisely to bribe him and to be able to say: "The reds say we are
eactionaries, but look, we are letting Diego Rivera paint all the hammer and
ckles he wants on public buildings." Do you see the ambiguity of his position? I
hink his going out of the party will do more harm to him than to the party. He
ill be considered a traitor. I need not add that I shall look upon him as one too
nd from now on all my contact with him will be limited to our photographic*

Portraits of Julio Antonio Mella signed by Tina Modotti, 1928
Collection: Comitato Tina Modotti, Trieste

Death portrait of Mella, by Tina Modotti, 1929
Collection: Comitato Tina Modotti, Trieste

Mella's typewriter, by Tina Modotti, 1929
Collection: Comitato Tina Modotti, Trieste

153

When Orozco visited the United States in 1927 and when Charlot arrived in 1928, each was required to make statements under oath, and perhaps this is what Tina was required to do by the U.S. ambassador. If she had been in possession of a U.S. passport this requirement was no doubt equivalent to the loyalty oath imposed on U.S. citizens as well as tourists and immigrants.

The question of a U.S. passport remains a very confusing one. She may have been able to obtain citizenship either through her father or through her husband. She made many trips to the States during the years 1923–32, if she did not hold a passport, then the Immigration Act of 1924 – the closing of the gates – would have affected her ability to travel freely between the U.S. and Mexico. As we know, the Exclusion Act referred to on page 144 would have made it more difficult to cross the border back into Mexico.

transactions. *Therefore, I will appreciate it if you approach him directly concerning his work. Hasta luego, dear.*

The importance of this letter lies not only in the information about Diego, wh had been considered the "Lenin of Mexico," but in the completeness with which it reveals Tina's strict adherence to Communist Party decisions.

It has been obvious from the tone of the editorial in *Excelsior* on the occasio of Mella's assassination that the political situation in Mexico had regressed and the gains of the last several years were being seriously eroded. The Sovi Union had been accorded recognition in 1924, but the attitude toward the Mexican Communists and political refugees from other countries had been getting progressively less sympathetic. Red-baiting, so blatant in the editori in *Excelsior* in January, 1929, had been spurred by the breaking of diplomat relations between the Soviet Union and Portes Gil's government in that year. The Communist Party was declared illegal; some of its leaders were slain, others jailed. Mexico was anxious to rid itself of the "fierce and bloody Tina Modotti." In February of that year a situation arose which provided the opportunity.

On Sunday, February 5, Pascual Ortíz Rubio was inaugurated as President o Mexico. After the inauguration, he left the *Palacio Nacional* to ride in the Bosque de Chapultepec with his family. Six shots were fired at him; they missed. "Although the youth (Daniel Flores – 23 years old) who had fired the shots was apprehended, all attempts were made to relate this crime to the wo of more intellectual people."

Tina was accused of being part of a conspiracy in the attempt to kill the President and was arrested. As a condition to remaining in Mexico, she was asked to abandon her revolutionary ideas. Imprisoned for thirteen days, she went on a three-day hunger strike in protest. At the end of this period she wa "administratively" expelled from the country and sentenced to deportation. S was given just two days to straighten out her affairs and even during that sho period her house was being watched by the police. The numerous protests of workers, peasants and intellectuals did not help her cause. But Tina was without a usable passport. Officially, American citizenship was available to I through her marriage to Robo, but she was not in possession of an American passport. Upon request for a visa to the United States, the U.S. ambassador, Dwight W. Morrow, offered one under the condition that she abandon her political activities. She rejected the proposition. At the Italian embassy she was also offered a new passport with the following notation – "valid only for a return trip to Italy"– sure death for an outspoken anti-Fascist. Finally she wa able to leave for Europe on a weather-beaten Dutch ship, the Edam. Before

She was to leave by train for the port of Vera Cruz, Manuel Alvarez Bravo, her long-time friend, was with her.

I learned that she was leaving and went to see her; I was the only person who was with her in her house. There were police; I don't remember well, but there were a lot of police — about four or five to take her to the station. She was still very agitated and very nervous. She was finishing putting her things in order so she could leave. Then, since she was throwing a few things out...well, with embarrassment I asked her if I could keep a few of the things she was throwing away (some of her photographs). She said yes; she told me smiling — she still smiled even though she was very nervous. She was always very polite and very friendly. Since I couldn't go with her in the same car in which the police and she were going, I went to the station. I got there first, and it gave her great pleasure to see me. I hadn't told her that we would see each other again in the station. She took a window seat and I sat down next to her in the train, and when the whistles blew I got off and waved to her from below. She was still very nervous but still in those moments of farewell she showed the same friendliness and warmth as always.

4

1930/1939 Germany, The Soviet Union, Spain

Street scene, Berlin, by Tina Modotti, 1930
Collection: Comitato Tina Modotti, Trieste

was no ordinary passenger ship on which she sailed; the Edam sailed from
Vera Cruz with Tina on board as a detainee. She wrote to Weston on
February 25:

*I suppose by now you know all that has happened to me, that I have been in jail
13 days and then expelled. And now I am on my way to Europe and to a new
life, at least a different life from Mexico. No doubt you also know the pretext
used by the government in order to arrest me. Nothing less than "my
participation in the last attempt to kill the newly elected President." I am sure
that no matter how hard you try, you will not be able to picture me as a
"terrorist," as "the chief of a secret society of bomb throwers," and what
not…But if I put myself in the position of the government I realize how clever
they have been; they knew that had they tried to expel me at any other time, the
protests would have been very strong, so they waited for the moment when,
psychologically speaking, the public opinion was so upset with the shooting that
they were ready to believe anything they read or were told. According to the vile
yellow press, all kinds of proofs, documents, arms and what not, were found in
my house; in other words, everything was ready to shoot Ortíz Rubio and
unfortunately I did not calculate very well and the other guy got ahead of me.
This is the story which the Mexican public has swallowed with their morning
coffee, so can you blame their sighs of relief in knowing that the fierce and
bloody Tina Modotti has at last left forever the Mexican shores?
Dear Edward, in all these tribulations of this last month, I often thought of that
phrase of Nietzsche which you quoted to me once. "What doesn't kill me,
strengthens me," and that is how I feel about myself these days. Only thanks to
an enormous amount of will power have I kept from going crazy at times, as for
instance when they moved me around from one jail to another and when they
made me enter a jail for the first time and I heard the slamming of the iron door
and lock behind me and found myself in a small iron cell with a little barred
skylight, too high to look out from. An iron cot without a mattress, an
ill-smelling toilet in the corner of the cell and I in the middle of the cell
wondering if it was a bad dream…They gave me only two days after the 13 in
jail to get my things ready; you can imagine how I left everything, fortunately
my friends all helped me so much; I can't tell you how wonderful they have all
been to me. I am still in a kind of haze and a veil of irreality permeates over
everything for me; I suppose in a few days I will be normal again but the shocks
have been too brutal and sudden.*

Two weeks later she was to write again, from the U.S. Immigration Station in
New Orleans:

*I cannot even remember when I wrote you last, so much has happened in these
last weeks and such unexpected things too — as for instance my presence
here — but — have gotten to the point where I just accept philosophically what
comes along. You know the old saying: "It never rains unless it pours"; well*

that just about fits my condition at present. I thought that after 13 days in jail Mexico City — followed by two days (all I was granted to get my things ready), and after being taken to Vera Cruz and put on a boat, via Europe, my troubles would be over — but no indeed — in the first place I learned that the boat employed one month and a half for a voyage that could be done in three weeks but since on this boat, passengers are accidental and its specialty is cargo, we stop at all the following ports: Veracruz, Tampico, New Orleans, Havana, Vigo Coruña, Boulogne Sur Mer, and at last Rotterdam. This would not be so bad i traveled as a normal passenger, but in my condition of being expelled by the Mexican government I am strictly watched in all ports and not allowed to touc ashore, excluding this port where the U.S. Immigration authorities brought me here, and here I am relegated for eight days, that is till the damned boat gets through its loading and unloading.

It was not just will power that Tina had; she also possessed that rare ability t stand aside and look with wry humor at her situation, commenting:
I hope, Edward, that you enjoyed a good laugh when you heard I was accuse of participating in the attempt to shoot Ortíz Rubio —"who would have thought it, eh? Such a gentle looking girl and who made such nice photographs of flowers and babies..." I can just imagine the comments of this order being ma by the readers of Mexico's yellow press on reading all the sensational "information" headed by huge titles on the front pages, calling me "the inquie Communist agitator," "the celebrated photographer and Communist," and so forth — El Universal *of Mexico City, among other things, published the following: "...in the home of Tina Modotti, the authorities found documents and plans which clearly indicate that her intention was to commit a crime similar to Daniel Flores on the person of our President, Ing. P. Ortíz Rubio; a her not having carried out her intention is only due to the fact that Daniel Flo. got ahead of her..." (Can you beat that?)*
The truth of the whole matter is this: The Mexican government was eager to expel me but they need a good pretext, so they took advantage of the attempt t shoot Ortíz Rubio and profited from that psychological sentimental-hysterical state which public opinion is full of during any public commotion — I am wondering dear if I have already written you all this — perhaps so — as I said before, I have forgotten when I wrote you last. The place I am in now is a strange mixture between a jail and a hospital. A huge room with many empty beds in disorder which gives me the strange feeling that corpses have laid on them — heavy barred windows and door constantly locked this last one — The worst of this forced idleness is not to know what to do with one's time — I read — I write — I smoke — I look out of the window into a very proper and immaculate American lawn with a high pole in the center of it from which top the Stars & Stripes wave with the wind — a sight which should — were I not such a hopeless rebel — remind me constantly of the empire of "law and order"

nd other inspiring thoughts of that kind —

The newspapers have followed me, and at times preceded me, with wolf-like greediness — here in the U.S. everything is seen from the "beauty" angle — a daily here spoke of my trip and referred to me as "a woman of striking beauty" — other reporters to whom I refused an interview tried to convince me by saying they would just speak of "how pretty I was" — To which I answered that I could not possibly see what "prettiness" had to do with the revolutionary movement nor with the expulsion of Communists — evidently women here are measured by a motion picture standard — Well my dear, I must stop now — the bell is ringing for supper — and the matron (who suffers from diabetes, poor soul) will come for me any minute to escort me to the dining room where she doesn't take her eyes off me for fear this "terrible radical" might escape her and infest the country with poisonous propaganda . . .

She concludes her letter with her assurances that she will forward an address in Europe — as soon as she has one — and adds her customary devotion to Weston sending as well a big hug to Brett.

"I am on my way to Europe and to a new life, at least a different life from Mexico," she had written. This unemotional reporting of her detention and expulsion, the matter-of-fact tone of her assurance of survival, is extraordinary in the face of the anguish Tina must have felt after being wrenched from what had been her home.

There is no erosion of will in this woman, in spite of her uncertainty about the future. She had been cut off from the three countries that had nurtured her — Italy, her homeland, to which she longed to return, the United States, and Mexico. She was no longer an individual who was an artist. She had become a political person. She was thirty-four years old, alone, seeking asylum, faced with still another crisis point in her life. What was the reality which gave her the strength to face the future? She had been strongly individualistic from childhood, never shirking the responsibilities which had been thrust upon her — indeed perhaps seeking out responsibilities had been a part of her character from the beginning. But she was essentially a private and not a public person. The tragedy of Mella and the exposure in the press and subsequent deportation had changed all that, but had not affected her perseverance.

When Tina finally arrived in Holland after a voyage of four weeks, the authorities there did not allow her to disembark. The Italian Embassy, acting on the authority of Mussolini's government, demanded that she be extradited immediately to Italy. The workers' organizations in Holland put the matter into the hands of a strong group of lawyers and at the same time demanded asylum for Tina. At last she was permitted to go ashore with orders to leave Dutch territory the same day.

Her comrades in the Communist party arranged for her to be admitted to Germany and she arrived in Berlin on April 14, 1930 — to a Berlin that was quite different from that William Shirer had once described:
From 1927 onward there was a general prosperity in Germany. A wonderful ferment was working there. Life seemed more free, more modern, more exciting than in any place I had ever seen. Nowhere else did the arts or the intellectual life seem so alive. In contemporary writing, painting, architecture, in music and drama, there were new currents and fine talents. And everywhere there was an accent on youth. One sat up with the young people all night in the sidewalk cafes, the plush bars, the summer camps...The old oppressive Prussian spirit seemed to be dead and buried. Most Germans one met — politicians, writers, editors, artists, professors, students, businessmen and labor leaders — struck you as being democratic, liberal, even pacifist.[1]

This was a Germany which Tina might have found conducive to making a new life for herself, but by 1930 all had changed.

The Wall Street crash in the United States in 1929 had drastically weakened the German economy. By 1930 unemployment was on the rise and taxation was strangling the people, especially the common working man, on whom the food tax placed the heaviest burden. The depression gave the Hitler movement its great opportunity, even though by 1930 the Communists in the elections had over four million votes and seventy-seven seats in the Reichstag.

Mr. and Mrs. Witte were among the first people Tina contacted in Berlin. We do not know who they were, but we know from Weston's Daybooks that they had visited Mexico in the mid-twenties and had purchased several of Weston's and Tina's photographs. Apparently Tina had remained in touch with them through the years, and they had always reminded her that they had a room already and waiting for her. "How can I praise sufficiently that exquisite and heavenly creature called Lady Witte? She emanates such a spiritual beauty that the best of one is stimulated by her presence," she had written. But Tina felt that she could not burden her friends and found a room, very convenient and private, where she hoped to live cheaply. She had no idea about remaining in Germany; she knew she had to make a living and she also wanted to be where she could be most useful to the movement. She wrote of her dilemma to Weston. "The idea of portraiture in Berlin rather frightens me; there are so many really excellent photographers here, and such an abundance of them, both professional and amateur, and even the average work is excellent; I mean even the work one sees in the windows along the street...I have been ondering if I could not work out a scheme by which to get a sort of income om the blessed U.S. Perhaps by contributing to periodicals, magazines, etc. I el that if Frau Goldschmidt gets around one hundred arks for articles in the New York Times, I should be able to do the same."

er reaction to the situation in Berlin was one of admiration for the Teutonic ubbornness and self-sacrifice in the face of economic stress. She noted at the people never laughed, but walked the streets very gravely, always in hurry, and seemed to be conscious of a heavy burden. Berlin had indeed anged from the 1927 described by Shirer.

he city itself she found very beautiful, even though "I have not seen the sun ice during my ten days here and for one coming from Mexico the change rather cruel. But I know that the wisest thing is just to forget sun, blue skies id other delights of Mexico and adapt myself to this new reality, and start, ice more, life all over..."

ne asked Weston if he knew some photographers in Berlin, and wryly ommented, "I well know of course that it is not good policy to look up hotographers if one is also a photographer, but all I would want from them practical advice as to purchasing materials and find a place to do some rinting, etc. If possible I never again want to go to the trouble of fixing up dark room, and I hope to be able to work in some dark room. If I was in the .S. I would become a member of the photographers' association and make se of their work rooms; perhaps something like that exists here. I shall see." a postscript she added, "I must beg you to divulge as little as possible my resence here. It might cause me trouble in the future. Thanks!"

ne wonders, however, if she did not know the great photographers who, from l points in Europe, were assembled at the Bauhaus during this period. he Bauhaus was the first great institute for design. By 1930 it had been in xistence ten years and was racked, from inside and out, by political tensions. lthough the director Hannes Meyer had dissolved the Communist cell of udents within the Bauhaus in March of that year, he himself was removed ecause of his supposed Communist activities (in his open letter to the Lord ayor Hesse of Dessau Meyer stated the futility of his assurances that he had ever been a member of any political party). Tina did not indicate that she et Hannes Meyer at that time, although we know that she did meet him later the Soviet Union. Their friendship was renewed in Mexico and endured ntil she died.

he work in photography produced by the Bauhaus masters would certainly ave surprised Tina for the innovative ideas expressed, and for their attitude

July 19, 1936 found Tina in Spain where she worked under the direction of the famous Canadian Dr. Norman Bethune. Her nom de guerre María was given to her by Acevedo, one of the founders of the Spanish Socialist Party.

toward the camera as an instrument in the service of a world where man had make peace with the machine. Artists such as Moholy-Nagy, from Hungary, experimenting in photograms; Piet Zwart, from Holland, working with collage Herbert Bayer, from Austria; Alexander Rodchenko, from the Soviet Union; were among the most avant garde painters-designers-photographers. Their wo went beyond that of documentary reportage and propaganda. Weston's work ha been exhibited along with Moholy-Nagy's in New York. Weston had extremely negative reactions to Moholy's experiments, and perhaps this kept Tina from contacting him and the Bauhaus group.

On the other hand, Weston and Tina were pioneers in Mexico. They had introduced photography as an art to a fresh and appreciative audience. In Germany and all through Europe photography had been acknowledged as art, widely practiced and widely appreciated for several decades. The Vienna Sal of Photography was held in 1891 (the work of Alfred Stieglitz was prominent in this exhibition). In Paris the First Exhibition of Photographic Art was held 1893. The Zurich Dada group had produced photographic abstractions withou a camera since 1918 and both Man Ray, an American working in Paris, and Moholy-Nagy, in Germany, were making rayograms by 1921. André Kertész, Hungarian living in Paris, was focusing his camera on unposed people and their surroundings, shooting, as he saw it, the fleeting instant. In Germany photomontage was an important device of John Heartfield, who applied it first to surrealism and later to political ends.

Perhaps all this had an intimidating effect on Tina and her photographic eye during the period of change and stress. By the fourteenth of May she joined the Unionfoto G.m.b.H., a professional photographers' association, and was issued a press card. But her photographic troubles were many, as she described in an undated letter.

I have been offered to do "reportage" or newspaper work, but I feel not fitted for such work. I still think it is a man's work in spite of the fact that many women here do it; perhaps they can, I am not aggressive enough. Even the type of propaganda pictures I began to do in Mexico is already being done here; the is an association of "workers-photographers" (here everybody uses a camera) an the workers themselves make those pictures and indeed have better opportunitie. than I could ever have, since it is their own life and problems they photograph. Of course, their results are far from the standard I am struggling to keep up in photography, but the end is reached just the same.

I feel there must be something for me but I have not found it yet. And in the meantime the days go by and I spend sleepless nights wondering which way to turn and where to begin. I have begun to go out with the camera, but nada. *Everybody here has been telling me the Graflex is too conspicuous and bulky; everybody here uses much more compact cameras...I have even tried a*

Landscape outside Berlin, by Tina Modotti, 1930
Collection: Comitato Tina Modotti, Trieste

wonderful little camera, property of a friend, but I don't like to work with it as do with the Graflex: one cannot see the picture in its finished size;...anyway buying a camera is out of the question...besides, a smaller camera would only be useful if I intended to work on the streets, and I am not so sure that I will. I know the material found on the streets is rich and wonderful, but my experience is that the way I am accustomed to work, slowly, planning my composition or expression right, the picture is gone...

I was advised not to give an exhibition till fall, that being a better time; by then I would like to have something of Germany to include.

She also noted with surprise that most photographers still used glass plates. The different standards of measurement confused her — "a hell of a mixed-up affair," she declared. This technical difference compounded the difficulty of language barrier.

I tell you I have almost gone crazy. I had to buy an enlarger apparatus and enough "tools" to work with. I did this unwillingly since I wanted to feel that I could pick up and go whenever I felt like it (or whenever I was forced to...) now I feel in a way tied down to my dark room...I needed to find a furnished room since I absolutely refused to invest in furniture also, and with another room next to it, with water. I underlined the water part because one ought to be in Berlin to realize the difficulty of finding rooms with water. At last I have what I needed: of course the furnished room is not fit for a studio, but since I am going to try getting along without making portraits, I don't need a studio.

Her unspoken fears and insecurities were always there to contend with, and she cautioned Weston in replying, "please *do not* put my name on the outside envelope."

A few days later, on receipt of a letter from Weston, she addressed him as "Dear 'grandfather,'" congratulating him and declaring, "if you had the little imp near you you would just play with him, or her, with the same precious youthfulness which belongs to you." And on another subject she states:

Oh how happy I was to hear from you. A few days ago I wrote you again but now I almost regret having sent it; I was in such a despondent state of mind and weak enough to not just keep it to myself and made you the victim of my weakness. Please forgive me, and do not worry about me; I will fight my way and the last word has not been said yet, and all these trials will bear some fruit, I am sure; in other words I have enough self-confidence and realize I must not undervalue my capacities. Only there are moments, who doesn't have them? when everything appears black (perhaps they are black and those are the moments of lucidity) but maybe next day the sun shines and the little birds sing and the panorama changes as if by magic!

These are words of a strong, courageous woman regretting her moment of self-pity for her solitude, and even able to add greetings to Sonia Noskowiak (then Weston's companion) and the boys.

Like all her letters to Weston since their physical separation, this one also contained "professional talk."

I was interested in your decision about the glossy paper. Yes, I can just picture the "pictorialists" lifting their arms in horror at this new "outrage" by this terrible terrible iconoclast Edward Weston! So far I have undertimed everything I began to make; this damned light after Mexico! And yet I had accounted for it; but I will know better in the future!

Apparently Weston had written to her about his reprinting of old negatives on glossy paper. These exchanges are fascinating, since it is difficult from Weston's Daybooks to see how the practically unbroken exchange of correspondence reveals the essence of their enduring friendship.

Tina had considered the camera as "the most satisfactory medium of registering life in all its aspects." She had already expressed admiration for the workers-photographers in Berlin. Germany, particularly Berlin, must have seemed alien to her Mediterranean eye and heart. In the few photographs we know from the Berlin period, we note that she could not function merely as a reporter. Without the time necessary to study and describe the social conditions around her, street life in Berlin seems to have brought out a touch of ironic humor and detachment in her. This can be seen when she observes the man and woman at the zoo and the nuns in juxtaposition with the nude statue (see pp. 170, 158). There was little she could respond to, little to evoke a human emotion or create the remarkably romantic yet accurate reportage which was characteristic of her work. Only in the landscape (see p. 165) perhaps is there a deep response to her new environment — to the verdant majesty and grand scale of forests so unlike the sculptured earth of Mexico.

Happily, at this time she began to meet some of the photographers and writers. When Lotte Jacobi, another fine photographer, showed Tina's photographs in a special viewing in her studio, one of the critics wrote:

The secret of her work was that she made the world visible by her vision — this vision meant that the sad eyes of a poor child might be more beautiful than that of a ballet-queen; that industrial landscapes, the means of production, the fields of sugar cane, rice, jars, hands, guitars, hats...are more beautiful than the green avenues of Switzerland. Only the men of this world are not happy. Why? This is the question one senses in her photographs.

He was obviously moved by Tina's profound revelations of the Mexicans' particular sensibility. He must have responded to her power to evoke a sense of place, of time, to be able to absorb her subject as though she had contemplated it deep within her and then was able to give it form. It must have been evident to him that Tina was unafraid of registering the honest sentiment she felt.

Essentially, Tina must have felt an unease in that turbulent year in Berlin. Although many of the German people were bound by their loyalty to defend the democratic Republic, Hitler continued to gain political support. The September election returns showed support of over six million, which entitled the National Socialists to 107 seats in the Reichstag, thus making it the second largest in the parliament. The Communists had also gained, their representation in the Reichstag increasing from fifty-four to seventy-seven seats.

But clearly the Nazis had captured millions of followers and were making headway in the Army. The elections marked a turning point; Germany was on the road toward the Third Reich. It was impossible to ignore the Nazi movement and the obvious transformations within German society. The deteriorating economic conditions, and the accompanying insecurity — since she could not as a foreigner find regular employment which suited her abilities — must have motivated Tina to leave Germany after a six-month stay. Besides, she had few close friends there. Her friends in the Communist Party particularly Vittorio Vidali, arranged for her to go to the Soviet Union, and she left Germany, arriving in Moscow in October, 1930.

Three months later (January 12, 1931), Weston received this communication: *I have been living in a regular whirlpool ever since I came here in October; so much so that I cannot even remember whether I have written to you or not since my arrival. But at any rate, today I received the announcement for your exhibit (just three months later due to the carelessness of the person who forwards my mail in Berlin) and I cannot wait one day longer to send you* saludos *with the same feeling of always! I have never had less time for myself than right now; this has its advantages — but also drawbacks, the main one being the utter lack of time to devote to you, for instance, if only through a few badly scribbled words. There would be so much to write about life here, but* no hay tiempo *— I am living a completely new life, so much so that I almost feel like a different person, but very interesting. Edward, as I wrote the above, I just got an idea, I swear it had never entered my mind before. Do you know of anybody that would buy my Graflex, very cheap? I could sell it here easily but the impossibility to get this size films makes it impossible. I need not add that it is as good as new and if you could find a buyer I would find the way to send it to you, people come and go daily. It has a Tessar lens 4/5 − 2 magazines, perhaps one can get one hundred dollars for it, and if necessary even less. I want to sell* *so as to buy me a Leica. Forgive this interruption. What I meant to say still is at I like immensely the short introduction to the leaflet announcing your hibit. So different and so intelligent! So at last New York enjoyed the treat of ur work! [at the Alma Reed Gallery] I wonder if you plan to remain in Carmel definitely? Dear Edward, if ever you feel you are in the mood for a few words me, the Berlin address is still good, only if possible, write compact, for many asons — How are the muchachos?*

d Sonia? My best thoughts to you all — Tina.

eston had indicated on the original of this letter — "Tina's last letter to me."

ie letter is remarkable for several reasons. She had stated, "I am living a mpletely new life, so much so that I almost feel like a different person." Had is new life become so all-engrossing and had she become so different that ie could cut off abruptly a channel of communication which had nurtured her r many years? Their correspondence must have been a lifeline for Tina, a idge between her, her photography, and the world of thought she shared with eston. Yet this was, according to Weston, the last letter he received from her. ie had never, in any of her letters, sought to proselytize him with her political eliefs, although she had always made it quite clear to him where she stood. ad he in his ever-growing dislike for "the masses" become tired of this change? She remarks, "If ever you feel you are in the mood for a few words me" — it is possible that his correspondence with her had lapsed. Tina as constantly on the move, but her family in California had heard from her, though unsteadily, until her death. Weston had known of her involvements ith Guerrero and Mella, as she knew of his liaisons. Had her relationship ith Vittorio Vidali meant so much to Tina that she could not continue her ommunications with Weston? She might have feared to involve Weston in a olitical situation; still, did she not feel in the rupture of her correspondence ith him a more aching sense of loss than in their physical rupture? These are iestions to which no one knows the answers, since no accounts exist to ilighten us. Accepting the fact that this was the last letter Weston received, it almost impossible to believe that it was the last letter Tina wrote to him.

lso remarkable in the light of later events is her desire to buy a new camera that she could go on with photography. And yet we know (at least we have evidence to the contrary) that she abandoned her camera some time ter 1931.

rnestine Evans, at the time an editor with J. B. Lippincott in New York, had ritten in February of 1931 to Jacob Doletsky of Tass in Moscow, "I have asked ina Modotti who is one of our best known American photographers to come d show you some of her Mexican photographs. I am certain that both you and

Couple at the zoo, Berlin, by Tina Modotti, 1930
Collection: Comitato Tina Modotti, Trieste

ress Cliché will be interested in her work. I think she ought to be using her camera during her stay in Russia." Miss Evans had been the editor for *The Frescoes of Diego Rivera*, which was illustrated with Tina's photographs, and was familiar with all of her work. Many Americans, among them Fred Ellis, an artist, and his wife Ethel, visiting and working in the Soviet Union at that time, had occasion to meet Tina, who was presented to them as a photographer from Mexico. She was apparently close to the people in the film world in Moscow, so that her reputation and work were known and acknowledged.

Throughout the twenties there had been creative ferment in Moscow, and it must have been important to Tina to discover the social context in which this ferment was born. Her own political and creative growth had taken place in Mexico, where the arts flourished at the same time that social progress through upheavals was gained. And her participation in both had produced works of tremendous impact.

On the other hand, the camera as a recording instrument was a dynamic challenge for the artists in the Soviet Union and quite different from Tina's approach to the camera, although she had made what she called propaganda pictures. We know from the work of Alexander Rodchenko, who had been at the Bauhaus, that experimental photography played an important part in the developing arts in the Soviet Union as early as the early 1920's; photomontage was used in magazines, in posters for both film and political purposes. Its great strength as a modern revolutionary expression made it appropriate for use on the agit-trains as they sped through the remote parts of the Soviet Union in order to reach the illiterate people living outside the larger cities.

Perhaps Tina was unsure and modest about her own work. She felt that photography had to be tied to one's own roots. Confronted with the great revolutionary experiment unfolding before her eyes, she may have decided that she had to become a participant in that experiment through her own education and politically-oriented work before she could again use her camera. She was not alone in Moscow. It was there that she resumed her friendship with Vittorio Vidali, whom she had originally met in Mexico in 1927. This friendship turned to love — a new love that was very closely identified with her own roots and her political passion for Italy and for the world. With Vidali's guidance, she became involved again with the Mezhrabpom, the International Red Aid in Moscow, as she had been in Mexico. The Communist Party also had offered her a very good job as a photographer but she refused it, choosing instead to devote herself to her own political education and to revolutionary activity.

Paul Strand, the great American photographer, has said that he always had an interest in the things that make a place what it is — not exactly like any other place and yet related to other places. Perhaps Tina too felt this and felt as well that a photographer's attitude toward life affects what her eye sees. Thus, perhaps it is not too difficult to understand Tina's decision to abandon photography. In Mexico and in the Mexican revolution, Tina had been a part of the revolutionary struggles. Her camera was her tool; she understood its every nuance. She felt deeply the struggles of the people and she identified with those struggles. She was too briefly in Germany, and perhaps Germany was too alien to her, for her to be more than an onlooker. She had indicated that she could not truly function as a reporter — her camera could not reveal what her being could not absorb.

When Lotte Jacobi visited Moscow in 1932, she renewed her friendship with Tina. Finding her so completely occupied with political work, she asked how Tina, a fellow photographer with similar devotions to the art of the camera, could so completely abandon her work. Tina explained simply but firmly, "I cannot use the camera when there is so much work to be done." This reply surprised Lotte Jacobi at the time but in retrospect (1974) she understood it. seems obvious from what we know of Tina that she felt she was born with an obligation to act — and that as a revolutionary, her commitment to the cause was her first obligation at this time. After all, she must have felt a great need to be part of that new reality which hopefully would point the way to reshape the world in her lifetime.

From that period onward, Tina worked for the Soviet International Red Aid — within the Soviet Union and wherever in Europe that organization could function. There is little doubt that not all of Tina's travels were in the service the organization, but that she also functioned on special missions for the Comintern. In abandoning the camera she had abandoned a career of almost ten years, during which she rose from a pupil and apprentice to the status of a recognized artist.

When Jay Leyda, the eminent American film historian, was about to leave for the Soviet Union in 1933, Alma Reed asked him to take the monograph of Clemente Orozco published in 1932 with an introduction written by her. She also begged him to take a large package containing Tina Modotti's photograph which she had been holding for some time. Leyda was much impressed with Tina's work and looked forward to meeting her in Moscow. He of course contacted Sergei Eisenstein in Moscow, who was sure to know how to locate Tina. At that time Eisenstein was completely absorbed in his great movie *Qu Viva Mexico (Thunder Over Mexico)*, which he made in 1931. He explained to Leyda that while he knew and admired Tina he had seen relatively little of her since he was protecting his Mexican film and did not want information about s friendship with Tina to filter back to Mexico or to his American critics. oth men studied the photographs Leyda had brought with him and both were pressed by her work. Leyda sought Tina out and found her living quite ntentedly in a small room in a Moscow hotel which was reserved for rty functionaries.

he appeared vivacious and apparently suffered no loss of freedom in the ny room she occupied," he states. How easy this is to understand! After the pulsion from Mexico, the brief though insecure stay in Berlin, Tina had deed found not simply a refuge but a home, physical and spiritual. In her w relationship with Vidali and her acceptance in party work she had und a security and a direction which must have afforded her the profound nse of peace she had been lacking since her expulsion from Mexico. eyda found that "there was no loss of political belief in Tina — she was almost onumental as a political worker as indeed she was monumental as an artist."

e believes that the decision to abandon photography at that time was entirely rs — she felt that she could not be both a political worker and a photographer. he had made a decision and this in itself restored confidence and hope for the ture, missing in her since the assassination of Mella.

y 1934 Tina left Moscow with the hope of settling in Spain and joining Vidali, ho had been there since the proclamation of the Spanish Republic in 1931. nce the fall of the monarchy, Spain had seen riots in Andalusia, monarchist ots against the Republican government, the rise of the Falange, the paratist movement in Catalonia, along with those early reforms which the epublic had begun to achieve. A program of agrarian reform, which meant e expropriation of some of the immense holdings of the absentee nobility and e Church, had been started in spite of the difficulties. The feeding, clothing d education of the young in secular (rather than religious) schools and the ght of women to vote, were among the early accomplishments.

ill, the young Republic could not change overnight a land which Pierre von ssen has described as "peopled with hundreds of thousands of monks, easure-stuffed monasteries and churches, and overcrowded jails, a land filled ith typhus and malaria; men and women dressed in rags. . ." Still the *Guardia ivil* shot down the strikers and were posted all along the roads and in the oods to prevent the hungry and poverty-stricken masses from attempting to cupy the seigneurial farms. Yet because the Communist Party of Spain, unded in 1921, was not yet a strong factor, it was not formally suppressed, d many Spanish Communists returned from exile. In spite of this, upon rival in Spain Tina was apprehended by the *Guardia Civil* and taken back to e border.

Edouard Daladier, then Premier of France, had had a brief flirtation with the left wing of the Radical Socialists, and undoubtedly it was in this period that Tina was permitted to enter that country. Settling in Paris, she earned her living by translating and continued her work in the revolutionary movement through the International Red Aid organization. She helped to organize demonstrations and aid for the victims of the Floridsdorf uprising in Vienna, those who had been able to flee after the betrayal of the trade union strike in February 1934*; for the exiled Asturian miners and their families after the revolt in Spain in November of that year; as well as for those French revolutionaries who were working to establish a popular front in France. (The Comintern policy from 1934 onwards was to establish an alliance of all left-wing parties, the working class as well as the bourgeoisie, to resist Fascism. It was at the Seventh Congress of the Comintern in Moscow in July 1935 that the Popular Front was formally voted as a policy.) She told friends that since she had come a little late to the movement, she had to work more diligently, tirelessly, in helping the many political refugees of all nationalities who were gathering in Paris during that period.

In 1934 Tina helped to organize demonstrations in Paris for Thaelmann, a German; Dimitrov, a Bulgarian; Rokosci, a Hungarian; Gramsci, an Italian; Mooney, an American; Prestes, a Brazilian; Ghioldi, an Argentinian; and for countless lesser known political emigrés of all nationalities. By the end of 19. Tina was able to return to Spain to join Vittorio Vidali and to enlist in the struggle against the continuing erosion of Republican Spain. The second uprising of the Asturian miners had, in October of the previous year, established the Union of Working-Class Brothers and succeeded in the creatic of a revolutionary Soviet throughout their province. Their revolution was completely quelled, as were the uprisings in Madrid and Barcelona, and civi war was inevitable.

After the October 1934 insurrection, a Committee of United Action was forme with the primary objective of liberating, through amnesty, 30,000 political prisoners. It was followed by months of intensive work and polemical struggle and the government had to call for new elections. On January 15, 1935, the Communist and Socialist parties together with the young Socialist and Communist organizations, the General Workers Union (UGT) and other group had signed the pact that created the Popular Front, and thus brought about th unification of the working class.[2]

Hugh Thomas has written of this period:
Observe how in February 1936, the two sides which by then had taken shape i Spain and which referred to themselves by the military word "front," put their quarrels finally to the test of the polls, and ... how the narrow victory of the

Popular Front had brought in a weak but progressive Ministry, regarded by its own Socialist and Communist supporters as a curtain-raiser to far-reaching social and regional change. The elections of February 16, 1936, gave to the forces of the left 269 deputies out of a total of 473 in the new Cortes; a clear majority.

Here were ranged the masters of economic power in the country, led by the Army and supported by the Church, that embodiment of Spain's past glory. All these believed that they were about to be overwhelmed. Opposed to them were the "professors" — many of the enlightened middle class — and almost the entire labour force of the country, maddened by years of insult, misery and neglect, intoxicated by the knowledge of the better conditions enjoyed by their class comrades in France and Britain and by the actual mastery which they supposed that the working class had gained in Russia. Tragedy could not have been avoided.[3]

On July 17, 1936, Vidali was returning from a trip to Paris to consult with some leaders of the Red Aid there, and upon arrival at the airport in Madrid he was informed by several of his comrades there to meet him, that the military rebellion had begun. The headquarters of the Madrid Red Aid *(Socorro Rojo)* were filled with comrades who had arrived there from all corners of Spain for a meeting to discuss organization. Vidali asked them to disband, return as soon as possible to their homes, and put themselves at the disposal of the Popular Front. Tina was already at work in the *Hospital Obrero* (Workers' Hospital), which had been abandoned by the Fascist doctors and religious nurses. Here she functioned as cook, director of personnel, and was ready to tend the wounded when they arrived. There in the kitchen of the hospital it was feared that the enemy might perpetrate a monstrous crime against the hundreds of wounded arriving from the Sierra. Simone Tery recalled how Tina said shortly before her death in Mexico, "'I shall never forget the arrival of the first wounded *milicianos...*.' She said no more, but I saw the expression of anguish in her face as she evoked that first contact with war." Tery had originally met Tina in Moscow, where she was known to her only as "María," and later in Spain and Mexico.

The famous Fifth Regiment was founded and commanded by Vittorio Vidali, known in Spain by his *nom de guerre*, Carlos Contreras. Tina enlisted in the Fifth Regiment, and worked with the International Brigade, made up of Communist and non-Communist volunteers, which had become the main work of the Comintern. She was active on the front, in cities and villages which had to be evacuated, on the roads organizing help for the soldiers and refugees. She also continued her work as a reporter — not as a photographer — for *Ayuda*, a weekly newspaper edited by the Red Aid of Spain, as well as for the Children's Home. She was known to all only as "María." And

Two letters have come down intact. One
written in November 1936 in which Tina wrote
to her mother apologizing for the erratic
correspondence; one from Tina to her sister
Mercedes in December of that same year
acknowledging receipt of the information of the
death of her mother. Each was written from
Spain and posted from Paris.

she worked especially with the first Italian volunteers — refugees who formed themselves into the Gastone Sozzi Battalion — men and some women who were of no particular political grouping.

Later the Garibaldi Battalion of the International Brigade, composed of all the left-wing parties, attacked the Italian Fascist infantry at Brihuega, outside the Madrid highway, but at first the Garibaldi men used this occasion to urge through loudspeakers and leaflets that *fratelli nostri* (our brothers) desert the Nationalist cause. If they came with their arms there would be an extra financial reward! It was the Italian prisoners who willingly talked about the extent of Italian intervention in the war.

Margarita Nelken, writer and deputy to the *Cortes* in Spain, later wrote: *For good, for absolute good, without restrictions or reservations, she was a revolutionary — a revolutionary in the most hidden fibers of her being...Tina Modotti, day by day during years and years without defenses to facilitate the sacrifice, lived under this sign: TO SERVE. She served in an exemplary way, to the prisoners, to the children who in the war needed a little food and much love; to the survivors of Málaga — who on the road to Almería were followed by cannon fire from German ships and bombs from Italian planes. Those who in Madrid in November of 1936 were together will never forget how Tina, surrounded by rubbish, bodies and dismembered limbs, how busy, diligent and serene she was in attending those most badly wounded.* [4]

It was in Madrid that she received the news of the death of her mother, and we can imagine her anguish at being so far away from her family to which she was devoted. In the spring of 1937 Tina was in Valencia for a Congress for the Defense of Culture Against Fascism. Among those attending were people like André Malraux from France and Pablo Neruda from Chile. Also present was a group of Mexicans, the poets Juan de la Cabada and the very young Octavio Paz; Silvestre Revueltas, musician; Angélica Arenal de Siqueiros, the wife of David Alfaro Siqueiros who was also in Spain, came to attend the conference and met Tina there. She had not known her during the previous years in Mexico. "For me," Angélica recalls, "there was a romantic aura about Tina. I had heard much of her history from David himself. She was the first person I met in Valencia. I found her very thin, still very beautiful, and very feminine. We did not talk of Mexico, nor of Tina's photography, because we were both immersed in what we each felt was an historic moment." Juan de la Cabada also remembers meeting her at that time — he had known her in Mexico in the twenties — and recalls that she seemed very pale, "talking but a little in a low-pitched voice; that lovely Spanish with the Italian lilt which added to its charm."

"How well I remember Tina in Mexico," Fernando Gamboa reminisced recently

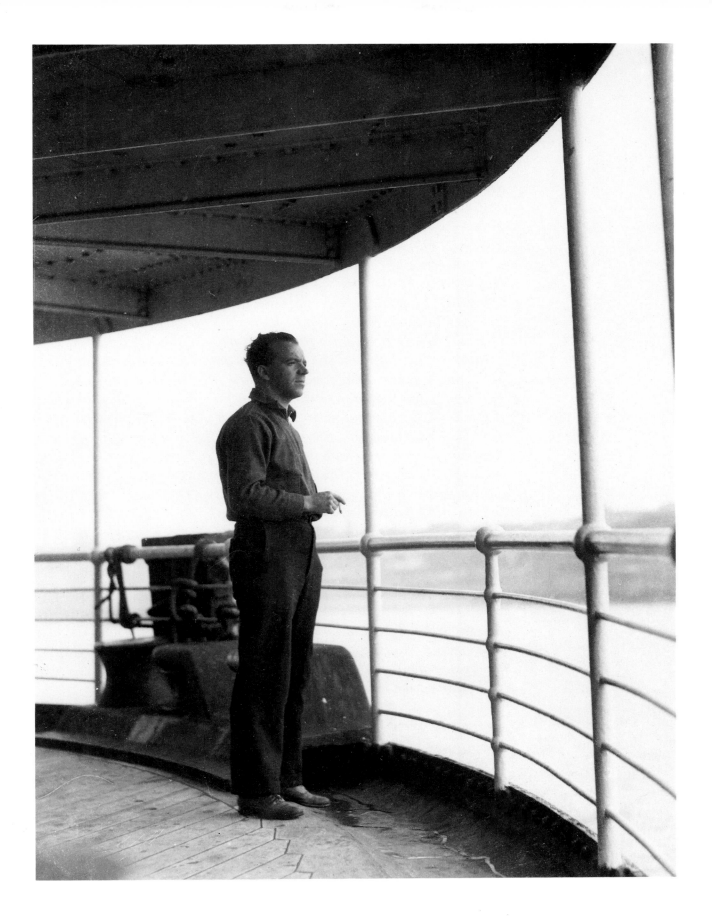

*Of course the "actress" syndrome of the 1920s was even more effective in Mexico than in the United States during the "Jazz Age," with its implications of immortality and sexual freedom.

In fact I remember her perfectly, when I first met her in 1929, with her hair tied at the back, her bright large sad eyes — her eyes were always shining but at the same time there was a melancholy look in them. She wore low-heeled shoes, a simple blouse and a black or blue skirt. She was loving and cordial, with a sweet, low voice and very affectionate. Everyone whom she considered her friend or comrade was treated with lots of care and love. When I first met her — I of course knew who she was — I was very young, but she was a woman who had already struggled a lot and participated in many things. She was a foreigner and she was surrounded by a kind of halo. The photograph which Weston made of her — it is like a symbol of Tina's personality and I am deeply touched by it (see p. 60). Tina sitting in a doorway...I think she was always a woman with a tragic sense of life, even though she knew how to laugh and to be happy. She had been oppressed, she had suffered humiliation. Her enemies said awful things about her. She was very beautifully Italian, lovely skin, jet black hair, a woman besieged by men. Many women know how to handle men who surround them. The miserable enemies are those men who do not obtain what they want and because of this rejection they put the woman down and say ugly things about her...She was a woman who had come from the United States where we know she lived a life like many other young girls who had been in glamorous Hollywood during that period.* I think it was an infamy and a calumny to say that Tina was an easy woman. She was like so many others, some of them Mexican women who followed her example. There was a kind of beauty and personality that was fashionable during that period — if we are right in remembering that the Soviets created a style that they called the proletarian beauty, all simplicity, without any make-up.

I didn't see her again until I met her during the Spanish Civil War. That was in 1937. A group of Mexicans were invited to the Congress for the Defense of Culture Against Fascism held in Valencia. I met Tina at the offices of the newspaper Ayuda. I had been familiar with her life up until the time of her expulsion from Mexico and I never imagined we were going to meet again so unexpectedly. I recognized her sooner than she did me; it was, after all, a long time since we had last met. I asked after her health and of course inquired about her work — she explained that she was working more as a correspondent than as a photographer and was very much on the move.

By the spring of 1938, it appeared to the outside world that the war in Spain was over. The leaders of Republican Spain were in exile, and France and England had given official recognition to the Nationalists. However, Herbert Matthews states categorically that "the Spanish Civil War ended on April 1, 1939."[5]

The Red Aid newspaper *Ayuda* was still being published in Madrid in August 1938; there were many still fighting the cause of the Loyalists. Catalonia

...ad been cut off from Madrid for many months and communication was almost impossible. Yet on November 1, a National Congress of Solidarity took place in Madrid. Twelve-hundred delegates — among whom were Socialists, Communists, Anarchists, Republicans, those without parties, men and women, civilians and soldiers — had come together. This was a union of the front with the rear guard, of the battlefield with the factory and the land, of the people with their government. The Congress was opened before an international delegation. Meanwhile aid came in the form of food and clothing through the new free roads open to Madrid. The enemy shelled the city that night. It was one of the most tragic of the war; Tina went from hospital to hospital looking for her friends and helping them receive proper care. Among the wounded, with grave injuries, was her own companion Carlos Contreras.[6]

Tina had never remained in one place; she had been in Pozoblanco when the whole of Andalusia was under the threat of the invader; in Valencia when the fate of that city was uncertain; in Caspe at the time of the disaster of the Aragón front (1937); in Lérida and in Barbastro when the enemy was besieging Barcelona (March 1938); in Extremadura when the enemy broke through the Republican lines; in the retreat from Catalonia when the army withdrew to the border covering the tragic exodus of the population. In fact, Fernando Gamboa recalls:

I didn't see her again until the army retreat...I was one of the last Mexicans to leave Spain with the great Catalonian retreat; we left with Col. Adalberto Tejada, the Mexican Ambassador at that time — he behaved so bravely in Spain. I had been informed that a very important hidden archive of tapes and films had been left at the Castillo de Figueras. My wife (at that time) and I were given use of the Mexican Embassy car. Everything had been bombed the day before because the last Cortes of the Second Spanish Republic had been held in Figueras and the people who were leaving Barcelona were pouring into the city even though the franquistas *bombed the city as well as the people who were on their way to France. It must have been in February. I went to the Castle, an enormous Gothic building, probably of the thirteenth or fourteenth century, and we found tapes and film, but actually this was unused material and not what we were looking for. I headed for another town nearby — about twenty minutes by car — but the town was nearly empty and I could not find what I was looking for. So I went to the center, and there, to my surprise, sitting alone at one of those outdoor coffee shops, was Tina. I asked, "What are you doing here?" "Just waiting," she replied. We embraced affectionately. She was waiting for the army which was on its way to that small town and she knew that Carlos was coming with it. I told her that she was in great danger and that she could not go along with the army — I even added as a joke, you are not in Mexico, you can't be a soldadera (camp follower). I tried to persuade her to come with me — the car we had at our disposal was large and carried the Mexican flag — in a half hour we*

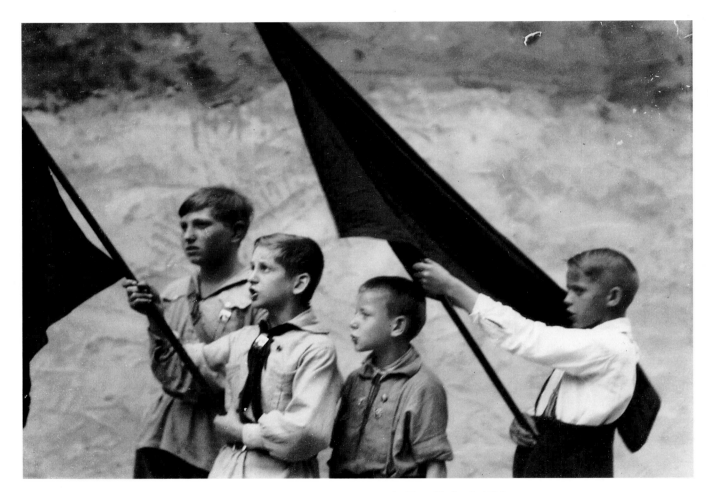

Young pioneers in the Soviet Union, by Tina Modotti, 1932
Collection: Comitato Tina Modotti, Trieste

...uld be in Guyana, which was where the embassy was set up; many people had
...one through there already. I see her now — a different Tina — a tired woman;
...he was feeling the agony of the defeat, she realized what the disaster of the
...epublic meant, the Republic for which she had worked and fought. Even I,
...ounger than Tina, strong and not tired, was in a very different situation. I was
... Mexican who was trying to help, but she was in the same situation as the
...paniards and foreigners who were there to fight and were now
...ispossessed — without a country, defeated, and obliged to run away. Well, she
...efused my offer firmly; I wished her luck; I sent my greetings to Carlos and
...oped that I would see them both again. I left, it was more or less at about six
... the evening, the sun was shining but gave no warmth. The whole scene, the
...ntire situation reinforced by the winter sun, the peasants escaping from the
...ountains, the army retreating and the image of Tina, sitting alone, with that
...aiting, searching, contemplative look — it seems to me that it is like the
...hotograph which Weston made of Tina in Mexico — sitting alone and waiting...

...nd so Tina became one of thousands of refugees who, with a perfectly valid
...lse passport declaring her to be Carmen Ruiz Sánchez, left Figueras,
...pain, with a visa from the Agence Consular de France. After seven weeks of
...ving in camps, she went to Paris and there received a visa to leave for
...exico, which had aligned itself with the Republican cause and which opened
...s frontiers to refugees from Spain regardless of their nationality. She had
...so been given a transit visa allowing her to stay in the United States from the
...me of her arrival on April 16 until the end of June. When the Queen Mary
...rived in New York, both Carlos Contreras and her sister Yolanda were there
... meet her. But transit visa not withstanding, Tina was not allowed to
...isembark. She arrived in Vera Cruz, Mexico, on April 19, 1939 — almost a
...ecade after she had been expelled.

5

1939/1942 Refuge in Mexico

The Mexico to which she returned was both familiar and yet strange. The pain of exile was to be borne not only by those who were political refugees from Spain and Italy but also by those from all the European countries who were the victims of Nazism. Mexico was at once a haven for the broadest spectrum of nationality and political definition: leftists of all persuasions, as well as active Nazis, Fascists and Franco supporters.

The political ferment of the entire world in this pre-World War II period was to be felt in Mexico. It seemed as though the suspicions, quarrels, retributions from abroad were being re-enacted in Mexico. It is normal for exiles to unite, particularly with language as a bond. But the quarrels and recriminations among the refugees from the Spanish Civil War became almost unbearable and the situation had become so muddled that one could hardly distinguish friend from foe.

Once in Mexico and reunited with Carlos Contreras, who had arrived there before Tina (he kept his *nom de guerre* all through his stay in Mexico), she earned a living by translating, while Carlos worked for the Communist newspaper *El Popular*. She lived quietly, and continued her political activities through the Anti-Fascist Alliance Giuseppe Garibaldi. She remained convinced that while she loved Mexico, Italy was her country. She always planned to return there after the defeat of Fascism, which she felt sure would come in her lifetime. They had close and trusted friends in Mexico, among whom were Verna Carlton and Ignacio Millán, Hannes Meyer, the architect who had been in Germany as director of the Bauhaus, Simone Téry, Pablo and Dalia Neruda. With these friends they would spend quiet evenings discussing the political situation abroad or listening to music.

It was not in the character of this honest woman to live under an assumed name in a country she loved. "María," as she had been called in Spain by all who knew her, was her *nom de guerre,* and she was proud of it. But Carmen Ruiz Sánchez had no reality at all. Through the intervention of the same Adalberto Tejada who had helped her in Spain, she was able to regain the use of her own name, and it was through Tejada's interest and intervention that the government of Lázaro Cárdenas annulled the expulsion of 1930. Tina proudly resumed her name and with it, interestingly, she returned to the camera. Mexico itself had changed, but the country outside of Mexico City must have struck a responsive chord and she was eager to accept an assignment. In Cárdenas' Mexico of the early 1940's, Tina's political life had probably reached another turning point. Perhaps she did not now feel the need to subordinate her work in photography to political action. In any case, her political activity must have diminished in Mexico, where the battle for the revolution seemed to have been submerged in the larger battles raging throughout the world.

Therefore, her return to the camera at this time is understandable.

For a book which was to have been written by Constancia de la Mora, another Spanish refugee, she went off again to record with her own vision and sensitivity the arts and crafts of Mexico and the people who produced them in their own environment. Alas, the book never appeared and the negatives have vanished.

Among the friends who had known her in the past and who saw her on occasion at this time, Fernando Gamboa states:

Tina is a wonderful example of the personality of a woman during that most difficult period in world history. There is no doubt that she was a great artist – her photographs reveal this – with an extraordinary sensibility, an exquisite, clear vision. If she was not an intellectual in the literary sense of the word, she was a woman forged by universal discipline; she was obviously an intellectual, as any real artist has to be. Even though Weston had great influence in shaping Tina's artistic vision, her photographs are in no sense similar to Weston's. He had a very different sense of space, he had an extraordinary technique, a whole sense of composition. Tina's photographs show a kind of human obsession, and her tragic sense of life can be seen in her work.
When I last saw Tina – here in Mexico right after the day on which the United States declared war – she was so tired, she seemed so ill, her skin seemed grey and spotted.

It is hardly surprising that Tina – her energies and emotions diminished by the hardships of the last years – appeared tired.

Hannes Meyer best describes Tina's last evening:

"Arrivederci," she said to me with a handshake. *That was on January 5th (1942) at midnight, as she left my house. We all – three married couples – had been talking for hours about everything we admired: the genius of Simeon Timoshenko, the Soviet anti-tank trenches, Shostakovich's Quintet Op. 57... and discussing the possibility of a trip from Madrid, Geneva and Udine to Moscow...without passports.* "Arrivederci," *she said again with a smile, and disappeared quickly into the dark night.*
Ten minutes later she was in a taxicab, motionless, cold, alone. Alive when she took the cab, dead when she was taken out of it....

Carlos had left the dinner party somewhat earlier in the evening to go to the office of *El Popular* before he planned to join Tina at home. She took a taxi and was alone when the tragedy occurred – a massive heart attack took her life. The driver was terrified, and abandoned the taxi; the police then brought her to the *Cruz Verde* (Green Cross), where friends came later to identify the body.

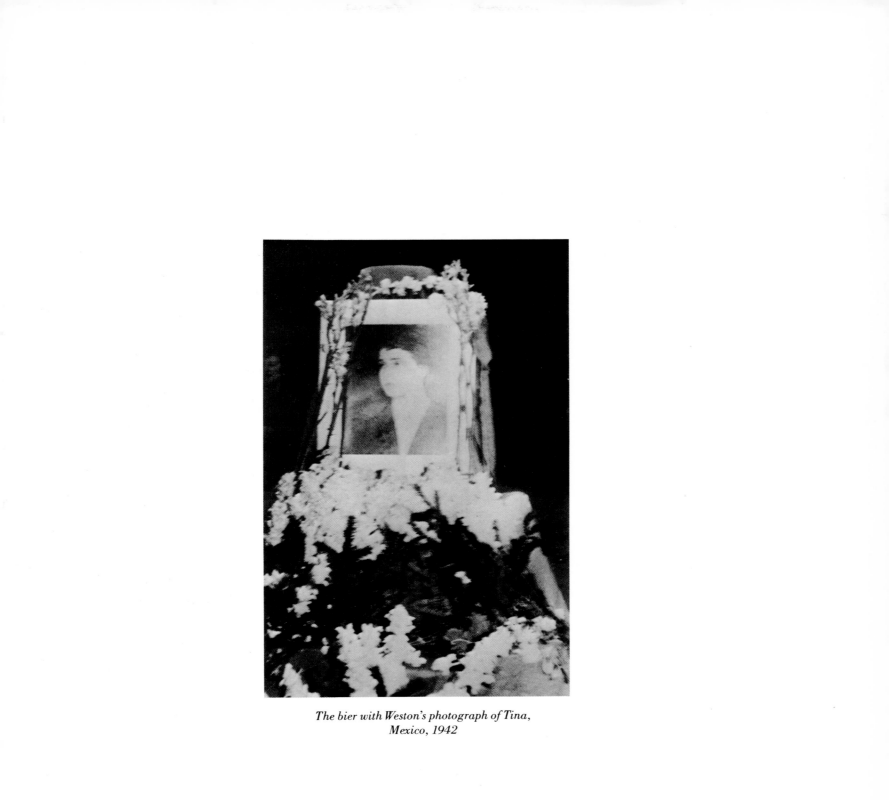

The bier with Weston's photograph of Tina,
Mexico, 1942

Tina's funeral, Mexico, 1942

death as in life Tina became headline news, and the calumny continued. [Sh]e became the victim of unjust accusations; gossip mongers speculated freely. [It] was rumored that she had been poisoned, and some even claimed that the [po]ison had been administered by her own friends. It was whispered that she [kn]ew too much about the still unresolved assassination of Mella. It seemed [im]possible that she would not be touched by the jungle of suspicion and rage [th]at was Mexico in that fateful year, 1942. The stories of her expulsion were [re]vived, and the rumors went on unabated, but as Margarita Nelken had said, [N]othing elevates so much as the attack of the enemy — there is no crown more [s]plendent than that of thorns."

[Un]known to most people but known to Carlos was the fact that Tina had had a [sli]ght history of heart difficulties while in Europe. Alvarez Bravo discounts [th]e rumors of poisoning. He quite easily accepts the fact that after a heavy [m]eal Tina suffered coronary failure due to indigestion and, given the lack of [m]edical knowledge in that time with regard to heart treatment, she died before [m]edication could be given.

[No]thing, it seems, stood between Tina and the pursuit of the astonishing goals [sh]e set for herself — only her own death, which was mourned wherever her [lif]e and struggles were known. The funeral was attended by thousands: close [fri]ends and comrades, workers, representatives of trade unions, women's [gr]oups, and government officials, who followed her flower-covered casket (with [th]e photograph of Tina by Weston) to the Pantheon of Dolores in Mexico, [wh]ere she is buried.

[O]n February 23, 1942, a posthumous homage took place in the *Teatro del [Pu]eblo*, followed by an exhibition of her photographs at the *Inez Amor Galería [de] Arte*. On this occasion Manuel Alvarez Bravo, her long-time friend and [fel]low photographer, wrote:
[Mo]re than by death, Tina's work was cut short by the fact that her life had [go]ne in other directions; still, in the short time that she was an active [ph]otographer, she was able to create a body of work which remains the lesson of [he]r understanding and her love of the methods and orientation most appropriate [to] the field…She combined human document, technical maturity, plastic surety, [ma]stery of her medium; all these brought together in this exhibition, which is [bo]th a stimulus and an homage.

[At] the same time, a brochure was published in which many wrote their tributes [to] her. For this occasion, and dedicated to Carlos Contreras, the Chilean [Pa]blo Neruda wrote his poem "Tina Modotti has died," which contains the [es]sence of Tina:

The myths abound and only sometimes they fade in the face of facts: one had her murdered in Rumania; another a suicide in Paris, but the following letter deserves to be quoted.

Nancy Newhall, a close friend of Edward Weston, who also was in part responsible for the Weston exhibition at the Museum of Modern Art, N.Y. (1946) wrote on May 27, 1946:
"Tina is dead. I have always meant to put in order the stories Edward and many others have told me. Fabulous stories; she must have been one of the most vital and exciting figures in those stirring times. Briefly, as I remember, she became more and more involved in the revolutionary movement in Mexico, married a revolutionary leader, Julio Antonio Mille, who was shot and killed in Cuba, was indicted for his murder and, with the artists violently testifying and agitating for her, was acquitted. Was deported from Mexico as a Communist, and after many difficulties, succeeded in landing in Holland. For the next several years she seemed definitely to have worked in the Communist underground. She was in Russia during the early thirties; was expelled from Spain, but returning during the Revolution. After the fall of the Republic, she fled to her native Italy when she died, very suddenly and not without suspicions of foul play, in 1942. Her memory still lies heavy as a charm on the people who knew her."

189

Tina's tombstone, Pantheon de Dolores, Mexico, 1942

Perfect your gentle name; perfect your fragile life
bees, shadows, fire, snow, silence and foam combining
with steel and wire and pollen to make up your firm
and delicate being.

TINA MODOTTI
1896 – 1942

Tina Modotti, hermana,
no duermes, no, no duermes:
tal vez tu corazón
              oye crecer la rosa
de ayer, la última rosa
de ayer, la nueva rosa.
Descansa dulcemente,
              hermana.

Puro es tu dulce nombre,
    pura es tu frágil vida:
de abeja, sombra, fuego,
    nieve, silencio, espuma,
de acero, línea, polen,
    se construyó tu férrea,
tu delgada estructura...

PABLO NERUDA

List of Illustrations

Front and back spreads: Fiesta in Huichitlan, by T. Modotti, c. 1926
Tina and Mother, San Francisco, by E. Weston, 1922, *18*
Tina, Udine, Age 4, *20*
Benvenuto Modotti, Udine, by P. Modotti, 1915, *21*
Tina, San Francisco, c. 1918−20, *22-23*
Tina and Robo with his family, Los Angeles, 1921, *25*
Roubaix de L'Abrie Richéy (Robo), *26*
Tina and Robo at home, Los Angeles, 1921, *27*
Tina in Hollywood, 1920−21, *28-35*
Roubaix de L'Abrie Richéy, by E. Weston, c. 1921, *37*
Tina, Los Angeles, by E. Weston, 1921, *38-41*
Assunta Modotti, by E. Weston, 1922, *42*
Tina, Glendale, by E. Weston, 1922, *43*
Self-portrait, by J. Hagemeyer, 1921(?), *48*
Tina, San Francisco, by J. Hagemeyer, 1921 or 1922, *49-51*
Robo's mother at his grave, Mexico, 1922, *53*
Yolanda Modotti, 1922−23? *57*
Yolanda Modotti Magrini, 1980, *57*
Tina, Mexico, by E. Weston, 1923, *56*
Tina and Weston, Mexico, 1924, *63*
Unidentified portrait, by T. Modotti, 1925, *66*
Anita Brenner, Mexico, by T. Modotti, 1925, *66*
María Marín de Orozco, Mexico, by T. Modotti, 1925, *67*
Xavier Guerrero, Mexico, by E. Weston, 1923−26, *68*
Edward Weston with his Graflex, Mexico, by T. Modotti, 1923, *69*
Drawing of Tina by Pablo O'Higgins, 1924 *72*
Drawing of Tina by Jean Charlot, 1924, *73*
Drawing of Tina by Diego Rivera, 1926 *74*
Virgin Earth and *Life and Earth* by Diego Rivera, 1925, *75*
Federico Marín, Mexico, by T. Modotti, 1924, *78*
Federico Marín, Jean Charlot, Tina Modotti on the azotea by E. Weston, 1924, *79*
Tina and Weston in the Marín family home, Mexico, 1924, *79*
Chandler Weston, María Marín de Orozco, Diego Rivera, Tina Modotti and Lupe Rivera on an outing, Mexico, *79*
Yolanda Modotti, San Francisco, by T. Modotti, 1925, *80*
Benvenuto Modotti, San Francisco, 1925, *81*
Tina, Mexico, by E. Weston, 1925, *82-84*
Tina on the azotea, Mexico, by E. Weston, 1924, *85-86*
Tina Modotti, Mexico, by E. Weston, 1924, *87*
Corn, Guitar, Cartridge, by T. Modotti, 1928, *92*
Rivera's *Lunch in the Rain*, by T. Modotti, 1926−27, *98*
Detail of a mural by Diego Rivera, 1923−28, *99*
José Clemente Orozco at work on his mural, by T. Modotti, *100*
St. Francis Helping the Poor by J. C. Orozco, Mexico, by T. Modotti, 1923, *101*
Architectural detail with murals by J. C. Orozco, Mexico, by T. Modotti, 1923, *101*
Crucifix, Michoacan, by T. Modotti, 1925, *102*
Head of Christ, by T. Modotti, 1925, *103*
Interior of church tower, Tepotzotlan, by T. Modotti, 1924, *109*
Staircase, by T. Modotti, *110*
Stadium, by T. Modotti, *111*
Telephone lines, by T. Modotti, c. 1928−29, *112*
Reservoir Tank #1, by T. Modotti, *113*
Convent of Tepotzotlan, by T. Modotti, *114-115*
Women of Tehuantepec, by T. Modotti, *115*
Easter Lily and bud, by T. Modotti, *116*
Calla Lily, by T. Modotti, 1927, *116*
El Manito, by T. Modotti, *117*
Roses, Mexico, by T. Modotti, 1924, *118*
Wine Glasses, by T. Modotti, 1925, *119*

sa, Mexico, by T. Modotti, 1924, *124*

man of Tehuantepec, by T. Modotti, *125*

man of Tehuantepec, by T. Modotti, *126*

man carrying anarcho-sindicalist black banner, by T. Modotti, 1928, *127*

z Jiménez and baby, Mexico, by T. Modotti, 1926, *128-129*

gnant mother and child, Oaxaco, by T. Modotti, c. 1929, *130*

by nursing, by T. Modotti, 1926, *131*

by, Mexico, by T. Modotti, c. 1926, *132*

chacho with sombrero, Mexico, by T. Modotti, c. 1927, *133*

xican girl, by T. Modotti, 1928, *134*

l carrying a pail, by T. Modotti, c. 1926, *134*

children, Mexico, by T. Modotti, 1927, *135*

sherwoman's hands, by T. Modotti, *140*

nds of a worker, Mexico, by T. Modotti, *140*

nds resting on tool, by T. Modotti, 1926, *141*

nds of marionette player, by T. Modotti, 1926, *142-143*

n reading *El Machete*, by T. Modotti, 1924, *146*

xican worker, by T. Modotti, 1928, *147*

ding bananas on a ship, Vera Cruz, by T. Modotti, 1928, *148*

gance and poverty, by T. Modotti, *149*

go Rivera addressing a meeting of the International Red Aid, Mexico, by T. Modotti, c. 1928, *150*

eting of the Hands-off Nicaragua Committee, Mexico, by T. Modotti, 1926, *150*

a accompanied by Diego Rivera on the way to police hearings, Mexico, 1929, *151*

traits of Julio Antonio Mella, by T. Modotti, 1928, *152*

ath portrait of Mella, by T. Modotti, 1929, *153*

lla's typewriter, by T. Modotti, 1929, *153*

et scene, Berlin, by T. Modotti, 1930, *158*

dscape outside Berlin, by T. Modotti, 1930, *165*

ple at zoo, Berlin, by T. Modotti, 1930, *170*

torio Vidali (Carlos Contreras), USSR, by T. Modotti, 1930−31, *177*

ng pioneers in the Soviet Union, by T. Modotti, 1932, *180*

a Modotti and Vittorio Vidali with friends, Mexico, 1940, *184*

bier with Weston's photograph of Tina, Mexico, 1942, *187*

a's funeral, Mexico, 1942, *188*

a's tombstone, Mexico, 1942, *191*

Bibliography

Note: the following is not an exhaustive bibliography but a list of publications which the author has directl quoted or consulted.

Brenner, Anita, *Idols Behind Altars*, Boston, 1970
——, *The Wind that Swept Mexico*, New York and London, 1943.
Caronia, Maria & Vidali, Vittorio, *Tina Modotti, Photographer & Revolutionary*, Milan, 1977.
Creative Arts, February 1929.
Dubos, René, *A God Within*, New York, 1972.
Dulles, John W. F., *Yesterday in Mexico*, Austin, 1961.
Hagemeyer, Johan, The Archive Center for Creative Photography, University of Arizona No. 16, June 1982
International Literature, Vol. 12, 1935; Vol. 1, 1936, Moscow.
Maddow, Ben, *Edward Weston: Fifty Years*, New York, 1974.
Matthews, Herbert, *The Yoke and the Arrow: A Report on Spain*, London, 1958.
Mexican Folkways, edited by Frances Toor, Mexico, D. F.
Myers, Bernard, *Modern Art in the Making*, New York, 1950.
Newhall, Nancy, (ed.), *The Daybooks of Edward Weston: Vol. I (Mexico), Vol. II (California)*, New York, 196
Niemeyer, E. V., *Revolution at Querétaro*, Austin, 1974.
Orozco, José Clemente, *The Artist in New York: Letters to Jean Charlot and other unpublished writings (1924—1929)*, Austin and London, 1974.
Radin, Paul, *The Italians of San Francisco: Their Adjustment and Acculturation*, Works Progress Administration, 1935.
Rollo, Andrew, *The Immigrant Upraised: Italian Adventures and Colonists in an Expanding America*, New York, 1968.
Rexroth, Kenneth, *An Autobiographical Novel*, Garden City, 1966.
Richéy, Tina Modotti, *The Book of Robo*, introduction by John Cowper Powys, Los Angeles, 1923.
Rivera, Diego, *My Art, My Life: An Autobiography*, New York, 1960.
——, *The Frescoes of Diego Rivera*, introduction by Ernestine Evans, New York, 1929.
Shirer, William, *The Rise and Fall of the Third Reich*, New York, 1960.
Thomas, Hugh, *The Spanish Civil War*, New York, 1961.
Vidali, Vittorio, *Il Quinto Reggimento*, Milan, 1973.
——, *Ritratto di donna Tina Modotti*, Vangelista Editore, Milan, 1982.
Von Passen, Pierre, *Days of our Years*, New York, 1939.
Wolfe, Bertram, *The Fabulous Life of Diego Rivera*, New York, 1963.

The Circolo Culturale Elio Mauro has published *Tina Modotti, Garibaldina e artista*, Udine, 1973.

CHAPTER 1

[1] Kenneth Rexroth, *An Autobiographical Novel*, Garden City, 1966, p. 344.

[2] René Dubos, *A God Within*, New York, 1972, pp. 122-123.

[3] Tina Modotti Richéy, *The Book of Robo*, introduction by John Cowper Powys, Los Angeles, 1923.

[4] *The Daybooks of Edward Weston*, Nancy Newhall, (ed.), New York, 1961.

[5] Richéy, *loc. cit.*

[6] *Daybooks*, Introduction.

[7] Ben Maddow, *Edward Weston: Fifty Years*, New York, 1974.

[8] Anita Brenner, *The Wind that Swept Mexico*, New York and London, 1943, p. 57.

[9] Bernard Myers, *Modern Art in the Making*, New York, 1950.

CHAPTER 2

[1] *Daybooks*, p. 13.

[2] Diego Rivera, *My Art, My Life: An Autobiography*, New York, 1960, pp. 161-162.

[3] *Daybooks*, p. 95.

[4] *Ibid.*, p. 101.

[5] *Mexican Folkways*, April–May, 1926.

CHAPTER 3

[1] Maddow, *op. cit.*, p. 49.

[2] *Daybooks*, p. 119.

[3] José Clemente Orozco, *The Artist in New York: Letters to Jean Charlot and other unpublished writings* (1925–1929), Austin and London, 1974.

CHAPTER 4

[1] John W. F. Dulles, *Yesterday in Mexico*, Austin, 1961, pp. 484-485.

[2] William Shirer, *The Rise and Fall of the Third Reich*, New York, 1960, p. 122.

[3] Vittorio Vidali, *Il Quinto Reggimento*, Milan, 1973.

[4] Hugh Thomas, *The Spanish Civil War*, New York, 1961.

[5] *Tina Modotti, Garibaldina e artista*, Udine, 1973.

[6] Herbert Matthews, *The Yoke and the Arrows: A Report on Spain, 1958.*

[7] Vidali, *loc. cit.*

Index

Page numerals in italics represent illustrations

Academia de Bellas Artes, Mexico, 52, 53
Agfa Paper Company, 145
Alianza antifascista Giuseppe Garibaldi, 11, 185
Allen, Sidney, *see* Hartmann, Sadakichi
Alvarez Bravo, Manuel, 14, 96, 97, 97n, 155, 189
Anti-Imperialist League of the Americas, 95
Arenal de Siqueiros, Angélica, 14, 176
Ayuda (Madrid), 175, 178
Atl, Dr., 53
Aztec Land Shop, 64

Bach, Fritz, 120
Bauhaus, Dessau, Germany, 163, 171
Bayer, Herbert, 164
Beals, Carleton, 13, 65, 97, 120, 120n, 145
Bethune, Dr. Norman, 164n
Brehme, Hugo, 97n
Brenner, Anita, 14, 52, 65, *66*, 71, 80, 80n, 81
British Journal of Photography, 145

Calles, Plutarco Elías, 78
Cámara, Pino, 123
Campbell, Gloria and Max, 120
Cárdenas, Lázaro, 19, 185
Carranza, Venustiano, 54
Chandler, Flora May, 44, 76
Chapingo Agricultural School, Mexico, 76
Charlot, Jean, 62, 70, *79*, 104, 104n, 154
College Art Association, 12
Comintern, 174, 175
Committee of United Action (Spain), 174
Communist Party, Germany, 162, 163, 168, Mexico,
    93, 95, 104, 104n, 105, 107, 108, 122, 151, Spain,
    173, 174, 175, USSR, 171
Contreras, Carlos, *see* Vidali, Vittorio
Cortes, Spain, 175
Covarrubias, Miguel, 137, 138
Creative Arts (New York), 13, 120, 145
Cristeros, 78
CROM (Revolutionary Federation of Mexican
    Labor), 78
Cuba Libre, 139
Cunningham, Imogen, 44, 78, 97n

Daladier, Edouard, 174
Daybooks of Edward Weston, The (Newhall, N.), 13,
    36, 55, 64, 80, 97, 139, 162, 167
de la Mora, Constancia, 186
d'Harnoncourt, René, 13, 77
de la Cabada, Juan, 62, 176
de Llano, Rodrigo, 138
Dewey, John, 77, 96
Doletsky, Jacob, 169
Dubos, René, 25

Edwards, Emily, 52, 81
Eisenstein, Sergei, 172

Ellis, Fred and Ethel, 171
El Machete (Mexico), 54, 93, 104, 105, 139, *146*
El Popular (Mexico), 185
El Universal Gráfico (Mexico), 12, 145
Evans, Ernestine, 169, 171
Excelsior (Mexico), 14, 106, 107, 120, 123, 137, 138,
    139, 154

Fabulous Life of Diego Rivera, The (Wolfe, B.), 151
Federal Arts Project, 12
Fernández Ledesma, Gabriel, 96
Fifth Regiment, 175
Figueroa, Gabriel, 96
Flores, Daniel, 154, 160
Florisdorf Uprising, Vienna, 174
Frescoes of Diego Rivera, The (Evans, E.), 171

Galería de Arte Inez Amor, Mexico, 189
Gamboa, Fernando, 14, 176, 179, 186
Garibaldi Battalion (Spain), 176
Goitía, Francisco, 53
Gómez Lorenzo, Rosendo, 14, 104, 105, 121
Gómez Robelo, Ricardo, 36, 52, 61
Guardia Civil, 173
Guerrero, Elisa, 62, 77
Guerrero, Xavier, 61, 62, 62n, *68*, 80, 88, 93, 96,
    104, 105, 122, 123, 136, 137, 137n, 138, 169

Hagemeyer, Johan, 45, 46, *48*, 54, 55n, 97n
Hands-off Nicaragua Committee, 78, 95, *150*
Hartmann, Sadakichi, 28
Heartfield, John, 164
Hernández, Galván, Manuel, 80
Hollywood, California, 19, 20, 26, 28, 45
Huerta, Victoriano, 53

Idols behind Altars (Brenner, A.), 80
International Brigade (Spain), 175, 176
International Red Aid, 160n, 171, 172, 174

Jacobi, Lotte, 167, 172
Jiménez, Luz, *128, 129*

Kahlo, Frida, 97n, 151
Kahlo, Guillermo, 97n
Kertész, André, 164
Kollantai, Aleksandra Mikhailovna, 20, 20n

Lawrence, D. H., 93
Leyda, Jay, 172, 173
Life and Earth (Rivera), 12, *75*, 76
Loyalists (Spain), 13, 178
Lunch in the Rain (Rivera), *98*

Machado, Gerardo, 104, 107, 108, 120, 139
Maddow, Ben, 14, 36, 47, 61
Magriña, José (Pepe), 105, 106, 121, 138, 139
Magrini, Yolanda, *see* Modotti, Yolanda
Malraux, André, 176

aría" (Tina Modotti), 12, 19, 175
rín, Federico, 14, 64, *78*, *79*
rín de Orozco, María, 64, *67*, *79*, 81
tthews, Herbert, 178
ther, Margarethe, 28, 45, 97n
Gehee, Ramiel, 28, 45
Partland, Neil, *see* Mella, Julio Antonio
lla, Julio Antonio, 11, 14, 104, 104n, 105, 106,
107, 108, 120, 121, 122, 123, 137, 138, 139, 145,
150, *152*, *153*, 154, 169, 189
ndez, Leopoldo, 12
rida, Carlos, 145
xican Folkways (Mexico), 12, 97, 104, 145
yer, Hannes, 163, 185, 186
zhrabpom, *see* International Red Aid
llán, Ignacio, 185
llán, Verna Carlton de, 185
dotti, Assunta (mother), *18*, 24, *42*, 56n
dotti, Assunta Adelaida Luigia (Tina Modotti)
dotti, Benvenuto (brother), *21*, 24, *81*
dotti, Giaconda (sister), 24
dotti, Giuseppe (father), 24, 25
dotti, Mercedes (sister), 24, 77, 176n
dotti, Yolanda (sister), 14, 24, 25, *57*, *80*, 181
holy-Nagy, Lazlo, 164
ore, George, 55
rones, Luis, 78
rrow, Dwight W., 154
seo del Estado (Guadalajara), 77
seum of Modern Art, New York, 13

tional Congress of Solidarity (Madrid), 179
lken, Margarita, 176, 189
ruda, Pablo, 176, 185, 189
utra, Richard, 97n
whall, Nancy, 189n
skowiak, Sonia, 167, 169

regón, Alvaro, 53, 54
Higgins, Pablo, 12, 70, 81
ozco, José Clemente, 53, *100*, 104, 104n, 154n,
172
ozco Romero, Carlos, 14, 64, 145
íz Hernán, Gustavo, 12, 14, 145
íz Rubio, Pascual, 154, 160

checo, Máximo, 104
acio de Minerva, 71
ntheon de Dolores, Mexico, *53*, 189
rtridge, Roi, 78
z, Octavio, 176
rgolesi, Gian Battista, 46
ular Front (Spain), 174
rtes Gil, Emilio, 107, 154
und, Ezra, 28, 88
ss Cliché, 171
aneda, Alfonso, 80n

e viva Mexico, see Thunder over Mexico,

Radin, Paul, 24
Ray, Man, 164
Reed, Alma, 172
Reed Gallery, Alma, 169
Revolutionary Syndicate of Technical Workers,
    Painters and Sculptors, 54
Revueltas, Silvestre, 176
Rexroth, Kenneth, 20
Richéy, Roubaix de L'Abrie, 26, *26*, *27*, 28, *37*, 44,
    45, 47, 52, *53*, 76
Richéy, Tina (Tina Modotti)
Rivera, Diego, 12, 13, 53, 54, 62, 64, 70, 71, 76,
    79, 80, 93, 104, 120, 121, 137, 138, 139, *150*, 151,
    151, 154
Rivera, Guadalupe, 64, *79*
Robo, *see* Richéy, Roubaix de L'Abrie
Rodchenko, Alexander, 164, 171
Rollo, Andrew, 24
Rosenblum, Isaac, 160n
Ruíz Sánchez, Carmen (Tina Modotti), 19, 181

Sacco, Nicola and Vanzetti, Bartolomeo, 94, 95
St. Francis Helping the Poor (Orozco, J. C.), *101*
Shirer, William, 162
Simonson, Lee, 120
Sindicato de Técnicos, Pintores y Escultores, 54
Siqueiros, David Alfaro, 12, 53, 54, 93, 150
Socorro Rojo, 175
Sozzi Battalion (Spain), 176
Spanish Civil War, 12, 13, 173, 174
Spanish Republic, 173, 174
Spender, Stephen, 174n
Stieglitz, Alfred, 164
Strand, Paul, 171

Talleres de Gráfica Popular, 12
Tass Agency (Moscow), 169
Teatro del Pueblo, 189
Tejada, Adalberto, 179, 185
Tery, Simone, 175, 185
The Tiger's Eye, 28
Thunder Over Mexico, 172
Thomas, Hugh, 174
Toor, Frances, 12, 96, 97

UGT (General Workers Union, Spain), 174
Unionfoto GmbH, 164
Universidad Nacional Autónoma de Mexico, 145

Varietés (Brussels), 145
Vasconcelos, José, 53, 62
Vidali, Vittorio, 11, 14, 94, 95, 137, 160n, 168, 169,
    171, 173, 174, 175, *177*, 179, 181, *184*, 185, 186,
    189
Virgin Earth (Rivera), 12, *75*, 76
von Passen, Pierre, 173

Weston, Brett, 77, 81, 97n, 144
Weston, Chandler, 61, 70, 76, *79*, 81

Weston, Edward, 11, 12, 13, 14, 20, 28, 44, 45, 46,
    47, 52, 53, 54, 55, 55n, 61, 62, 62n, *63*, 64, 65,
    69, 70, 71, 76, 77, 78, *79*, 80, 81, 88, 93, 94, 95,
    96, 97, 105, 138, 139, 144, 145, 151, 159, 160,
    160n, 162, 163, 164, 166, 167, 168, 169, 186
Witte, Mr. and Mrs., 162
Wolfe, Bertram, 65, 151
Wolfe, Ella, 95

X, *see* Guerrero, Xavier

Zwart, Piet, 164